# Freaks I've Met

## Donald Jans

ISBN: 978-0-9961756-0-9 (sc)
ISBN: 978-0-578-15215-8 (hc)
ISBN: 978-0-9961756-1-6 (e)

Library of Congress Control Number: 2015900297

Sheabeau Publishing rev. date: 3/20/2015

For Shealand and Beau Henry for teaching me what real love is...

With special thanks to anyone who has ever made
me laugh. I would be dead without you.

And to the late great Lee Beau Brown, thanks for the title.

# Contents

# Chapter 1

# May, 1987

Spokane remained one of the few cities left to live out the original American dream, complete with chivalrous cowboys and fast-food fed women who wanted to stay home and raise white children. That was boring.

If I stayed in Spokane, the slickest job I could get would be selling last year's shoes in the basement of Nordstrom's, with the promise of moving up to the main floor after five years if I kissed the right asses. I had done enough of that. I was convinced that the proverb about money not buying happiness was written by a rich guy who didn't want you to feel bad because you didn't have any. This way you'd stay working for him in the same silly job forever.

Don't get me wrong, Spokane had plenty of fun up its sleeve and more than its share of crazies to startle you from time to time. Like two summers ago, when a crazy vet chopped up one of the town's seven hookers from East Sprague and buried her inside his wife's pink Samsonite in his backyard. He might have even gotten away with it if his German shepherd hadn't dug up the suitcase while his wife was having the neighbor ladies over for happy hour.

Speaking of happy hour, if I could just get the hell out of here, I could make it down to my Cousin Barb's house in Medford before sundown for a free place to crash. That was the halfway point to my new life. California was the place to be because, as near as I could tell, New York was filled with a bunch of Roseanne Roseanna Dannas.

But I had just one last errand this morning before I got on my way. Mrs. Pohlkiss still owed me 250 bucks. I wish I could just let the old bitch keep it and never have to see her again, but that was almost half my cash, and I heard one drink in a bar down there costs as much as a twelve-pack of Rain Dogs.

# Chapter 2

# Sweet Good-Byes

I downshifted into second gear and roared up the coveted South Hill toward Mrs. P's house, taking a right on Cliff Drive near where we used to park, make out, and party, until the cops shooed us away. This view from South Hill was reserved for rich people in the megamansions built at the turn of the century by railroad and mining magnates. Spokane's economy hadn't recovered since, so now the mansions were mostly filled with people who didn't deserve them, like Californians who just moved up here and did nothing after selling their houses, and assholes like Mrs. Pohlkiss.

My tires crackled onto the graveled lookout of Cliff Drive for one last view of my pine-treed city. The trademark black spires of my alma mater, Gonzaga University, jutted proudly into the sky like the pointed black leather bra of a reclining dominatrix on her cigarette break. At night, the white crosses atop her nipples even lit up. She was always open for business. My mom was a secretary in the business school there, so I got free tuition, plus a little extra scholarship money for my good grades. I even got some money for being left-handed. Leave it to Mom to know about all the random scholarships out there. And trust me, she made sure I applied to them all.

Gonzaga took pride in instilling a solid work ethic in the Jesuit tradition: if you obeyed the Golden Rule, you were sure to get a good job working with nice people, and everything would work out just fine, you'll see. I didn't want *fine*. I wanted to be somebody. Somebody with

3

plenty of "fuck you" money, like our two biggest alums, Bing Crosby and megabasketballer John Stockton. They had enough money to have the confidence to walk away from something if it wasn't right.

But everyone knew to get that kind of money, you had to get the hell out of Spokane first. Then, if you made it, like got a part on a sitcom, showed your tits in *Playboy*, or published a book or something, they'd invite you back in May to treat you like royalty during the Lilac Parade by giving you a desirable spot rolling right behind the Lilac Princess and her court. Or if you wanted to be more low-key, you could dedicate a building to yourself at Gonzaga as a tax write-off and your name would live on forever in stone above the doors, like Bing did with our library. Or at the very, very least, you could show up in the bars around the holidays and let these small-town folks know just how sophisticated you'd become by wearing your new city fashions. Then you could grab your pick of the litter, which was usually someone who wanted out of town too, like maybe a former Lilac princess who'd been bumper-pooled around town too much, and was now desperate because there was no one left—desperate as that Vietnamese refugee reaching out for the dangling hand of the soldier on the last helicopter leaving Saigon.

It was my turn to do something big with my life. I slammed the Jeep into reverse and crunched out of the gravel pad, whirring backward down the quiet street like an air raid siren, all the way to the Pohlkiss place before skidding into her three car wide driveway and tapping out "shave and a haircut, ten cents" on my horn. It drove her nuts when I honked at her, because she was all sophisticated in her big fat house, but I was through giving a shit about what she wanted.

She knew I was here, but unless I knocked on the door, she'd make me wait at least five minutes before she'd make an appearance with big, wide eyes, all surprised, like it was just a coincidence that she happened to be walking to her front door, and I just happened to be parked in her driveway. Mrs. P was good at games, but I was better. While I sat tight in my Jeep waiting her out, I looked around the yard to admire my work one last time. I had done a pretty good job over the past several years.

The lawn was so perfect you could putt on it, except for the big brown patch over near the mailbox that I'd fashioned into the shape of an "M" in honor of my dog, Montana. It was nice to think of Montana whenever I needed to take a leak. If you ask me, she was getting off easy for killing Montana— my best friend, my everything—after Dad died.

"Jack? Is that you?" Mrs. Pohlkiss screeched, craning her neck around the door.

There she was, almost at the fifth minute, just like always. She sauntered through her custom glass storm door onto her massive front porch wearing a pleased sneer on her wrinkled face. I'll bet she'd been waiting for me all morning.

She patted her left breast and folded her other arm across the chest of her expensive brown conservative dress, looking like one of those hand-carved wooden Indian chiefs you can buy on the side of the road near the reservations.

"Did you forget something?" she asked, walking toward me.

Of course she was going to make me ask.

"Oh, yes. Sorry, Mrs. Pohlkiss, remember? The last $250?" She reached into her bra for the money. No burglar would ever look in there.

"Oh dear. I only have $200," she licked her thumb and counted out the twenties like she was doing me a favor. "But if you'll go with me to the bank, I can get you the—"

I politely snatched the warm money out of her hand before she could take it back. The banks weren't open for another two hours.

"No, no, that's okay," I smiled, tucking the bills into the tiny front pocket of my faded Levis.

I should have known. This was always her trick on payday, but little did she know that I would have paid her a hundred not to have to listen to her go on and on about her perfect fucking son, Charles, who got to go back east to Yale, and was now at Harvard in grad school milking a few more free years of money out of his old lady.

Growing up, Mom used to make me play with Charles because our dads were best friends. Back then, they were our neighbors, and they were poor, like us. Our dads were so close they even died together— some of the last soldiers not to make it out of Vietnam.

Everything changed after that. We hadn't had our government-issued-folded-triangle flag a week when Mrs. P came over screaming like a winning game show contestant. Turns out her husband had kept a big secret from her. She was the sole inheritor of a three-thousand-acre wheat farm south of Spokane that had been in her dead husband's family for over one hundred years. She sold it within a month of his death and bought this place on Cliff Drive. So much for nostalgia.

Mom and I still lived in Hillyard on the north side of town, in our two-bedroom house with the same scrawny elm tree that never seemed to grow, surrounded by all the people who never went to college and never moved out of Spokane.

Mom didn't like me playing with the neighbor kids in Hillyard. It wasn't because they were poor. It was so she wouldn't have to talk with the other mothers. Mom just kind of closed up after Dad died. She never even went on a date. New friends would try to set her up, and that just made her think about Dad, and she'd get sad all over again. So every day after school, she'd make me take the bus across town to play with Charles until she finished cleaning their house. That's right: Mom cleaned that asshole's house for six years before she got the Gonzaga job.

Even now, I could tell that Mrs. P thought she was better than us, and she let me know it whenever she could.

"How's your mother doing?" Mrs. P leaned back on her heels with her arms crossed, staring at the lawn. "She's such a hard-working lady." She shook her head like work was something Mom indulged herself in.

"She's great. You should give her a call."

Mom pretended never to buy into Mrs. P's bullshit, but I hated myself for letting her get under my skin all these years. And especially for taking away the one thing that made me happy after Dad died: Montana. For that, I would never forgive her.

I don't blame Charles for the dog thing, other than he existed that day. It wasn't easy having a mother like her, but he could be a real pain in the ass too. For starters, he always agreed to anything I said, which might sound nice, but it was a major pain in my ass. Sometimes I used to pin him down and fart in his face when I couldn't stand him anymore—until he started to like it, so I stopped.

But Charles wasn't all bad. Sometimes he would show me his mom's massive dildo collection that she kept under lock and key underneath her bed. One time we stole one of the biggest ones and threw it off the Liberty Park Cliffs onto I-90, just to watch it bounce. It got serious air when it first landed and rebounded up about six feet, but after the fourth sproing it got stuck between the wheels of a Rosauers big rig headed to Couer d'Alene and was never seen again. I can only imagine the trucker prying that big black dildo out from between his tires wondering where it came from. I didn't think Mrs. P would miss it because she had so many others, but I was wrong.

"You've taken something of mine; now give it back!" she screamed at Charles the next day while we were chomping down on our usual afternoon snack of Cocoa Pebbles, a ritual we were unwilling to give up from our kid days in Hillyard.

I did my best to look confused at Mrs. P, but my stomach churned at the thought of Mom finding out the real story. Charles got grounded for two weeks. I didn't know it then, but Mrs. P would have never mentioned the dildo incident to anyone anyway—too much of a prude.

I felt bad for letting Charles take the brunt, but it's not like I was going to drive to Idaho to search the Flying J Truck Stop for her mangled dildo. Plus, he would have gotten into *way* more trouble if she'd known he'd shown me her treasures.

I watched Mrs. P pace the perimeter of her lawn one last time. Did she actually think I was going to fix anything this morning if it was wrong? I could almost hear Montana barking as she headed toward the brown "M." She kicked the brown grass with her dark brown dress shoe before she hiked up her dress above her knees and got down on the lawn to sniff it with her pointed nose, forcing a smirk on my face.

"Must be the radon gas," she said.

Two years ago, she'd been scammed into installing a white plastic two-foot-diameter vent pipe in the cement floor of her basement. That vent pipe was the current cure drummed up by some hucksters to magically eliminate "radon cancer gas." Everyone knew radon naturally seeped through the volcanic rock that was everywhere in Spokane, but only "the pipe" could siphon the killer gas away from the loved ones of those who could afford it. Mrs. P had the deluxe model installed, which meant it had a small red plastic light that always stayed on, just to let you know it was working while you were out fucking around. Kind of like the lit-up crosses atop the Gonzaga spires.

"You sure have a lot of stuff," she said, following me back to my Jeep. She reached down and thwacked one of the black bungee cords that secured the blue tarp on top of my load. She shook her head one more time, judging my jam-packed Jeep like it was filled with shit. It was filled with shit, but it was *my* shit.

"What if it rains?" she added.

I stayed silent. *Yeah, so what if it rains? I'll get wet, but I won't have to listen to your crap anymore.*

"It sure would be a shame if you just had to bring it all back," implying, in her special way that I was going to fail. "There are plenty of jobs for young people like you in Spokane. Your mother has done fine."

My blood boiled but I clamped my mouth shut. This was going to be the last time she would ever put me down. I will make more money than she ever knew existed. I was never coming home. Mom could visit me in a private jet. I'd even pay the pilot extra to buzz Mrs. P's house on the way out of town.

"Well, thanks again for everything, Mrs. Pole Kiss." I said sarcastically. I only made her last name into two words whenever she made me mad. Nice ladies wouldn't even get the slam, but Mrs. Pohlkiss did.

She folded her arms again and shook her head at me. I slammed it into gear and squealed out of her driveway, leaving a final black skid mark to go with Montana's honorary "M."

Mrs. P hobbled across the lawn like her panties had fallen around her ankles, frantically waggling her index finger at me to stop so she could scold me one last time. Right now I wanted to flip her off—the final symbol that her abuse was over, but then she would have won. She'd call Mom, who'd make me apologize, *or else*, and then I'd just get angry all over again. Nope. This game was over.

# Chapter 3

# Graduate Disillusionment

I glanced in my rearview mirror at the top of Sunset Hill, and watched the stubby Spokane skyline disappear. I felt sad—as if I was dumping an old friend for a cooler crowd. And I was. I just needed to find them first.

I tossed my bulging wallet onto the dashboard and smushed my cowboy hat down extra low to protect me from the buffeting wind, and headed south through the endless undulating wheat fields, dreaming of all the movie star pools I might swim in once I got to town.

You see, I was moving to LA to become rich and famous. About a month before school let out, I was washing my Jeep down at the do-it-yourself spray gun place on Third. It was caked with six inches of mud from four-wheeling, and the last time I hosed it off at Mom's house she had a cow. Oh, I know what you're thinking. Four-wheeling is for mouth-breathers. But I need a break from civilization more than most people do to keep me sane.

So there I was on the hot wax cycle, shirtless, down to just my Wranglers, hat, and boots, when this chubby clean-cut guy in khakis and a pink shirt started checking me out. He was about ten feet from me, walking around the front of my car wash bay in his cordovan penny loafers with no socks. He was holding his hands out arm's length in front of his face to form a square with his fingers, looking through the center at me. It was pretty creepy, but I knew I could kick his ass if I had to.

Spokane has its fair share of tourists and all, especially in the summer, looking for authentic cowboys to go along with all the mountains and rivers where the deer and the antelope play. So I just went about my business and humored him, doing my part for the Chamber of Commerce. But I am no cowboy. Horses scare the shit out of me. And the hat and the boots? Well, they are just plain comfortable. Plus they're the two clothing items that are always on sale at the local stores.

"There's a rodeo this weekend out at the fairground," I said when he took out his 35 mm camera.

"Mind if I take a few?" he asked. I shrugged yes. He was getting kind of ridiculous taking pictures. But I couldn't help but smile, because he totally had the wrong guy. "I don't want the rodeo. I want you," he said.

He walked up to me and extended his overly tanned hand that went along with his fake-bake orange body. "Alain Michaels," he said, making it sound French. I shook his hand. It was like humid pottery clay. No one had ever taken the time to put him through handshake boot camp.

"Jack."

He handed me his card and said he ran a big modeling and talent agency in Beverly Hills.

"You have just the right look." He glowed.

"Right look for what?" I looked down at my muddy, wet Wranglers.

"I could get you working right away in print ads or TV if you came down to LA."

"Thanks but no thanks." I handed him his card back. I'd heard about guys like him who get you to come back to their hotel room for a "photo shoot" and then try to get in your pants. But just then, his beautiful blonde girlfriend in a tight red T-shirt came skipping down Third holding a white paper bag with a panda on it from Dick's Burgers.

"Alain! Lovey. They have homemade ice cream sandwiches for only twenty-nine cents." She walked up and handed Alain the bag before giving him a kiss on the lips. "It's so cute here. It's like time stopped." She stamped her white canvas shoes softly at me like she had to go pee.

"Who's this?" She held her hand high for me to shake in a very nasty sexy way. "I'm Lauren." Unlike Alain, her fake bake tan looked pretty natural and went with her peach-colored manicured nails perfectly.

"Could be the next *Greatest American Hero*," Alain said.

"He'd certainly fit the suit," she added.

"But he says he'd rather stay here playing in the mud," Alain mocked, folding his arms and staring at me.

"He's like a tall Robert Redford. Turn around?" she asked.

I obliged her while watching a cool breeze envelop her T-shirt. I'd always thought that being liked for your looks was about the lamest thing in the world, but her emerging rock-hard nipples made me realize it was time to grow.

I knew better than to tell anyone the truth that I was moving to California to become a male model. I didn't need anyone waiting for me to fail, so I told people who asked that I had a job in LA working with Dexter, my best friend from college. But I didn't even have the guts to tell Dexter the truth.

As I passed a green highway sign that said "Medford, 10 miles," the sun and the batteries of my Walkman were calling it quits on the day. I was excited to see my only cousin, Barb. She'd graduated from Gonzaga the year before and was already managing a Limited Clothing Store at the Rogue Valley Mall.

I parked in the fire lane so no one would steal my stuff, and strolled in through the smoked glass doors, eager to see Barb kicking some ass in the business world. Back at school, she never had a problem getting whatever she wanted.

I walked along the mall's shiny cool cement. Even though I couldn't afford it, I decided to splurge on two large Orange Julius drinks, complete with the raw egg, to celebrate my new freedom. Beers and bong hits would come later.

Inside her Limited store, I found Barb in the corner leaning back on a sweater rack like an old-timer in a bar, sighing at her teen employee, who was talking on the phone like a Valley Girl.

"Barbie Doll! What's up, cuz? You knocking 'em dead?" I reached both full hands around her to give her a hug. She didn't smile.

"How many neon wool coats can *you* sell?" she asked, grabbing her drink from me without a thanks and taking a long sip. Barb's confident sultriness, her trademark, an inspiration to so many back at school, was nowhere to be found. That scared the shit out of me.

"Omigod. There he is!" Barb held her drink in front of her face like an elephant hiding behind a birch tree.

"Who?"

"Chet."

She was too late. Through the glass wall I watched a bespectacled brown-haired dork waving his McDonald's bag over his head at us like a rocker at a Metallica concert. He spun a 360 on his black vinyl dress shoe.

"No one, no, oh, one, no one ever. Is to blame," Chet belted. The shop girls across the way at Casual Corner started pointing and laughing at him.

"I am actually almost fucking the assistant manager at the Deadford Mall Chess King," she whined. "Jack. What happened to me?" she asked, stomping her right foot. A pained smile crept up her face as she fakely twinkled her fingers at her new beau before he bounced into his own glass cage at the Chess King, waving his McDonald's bag one more time at her.

"Tonight, Barb! You and me!" Chet screamed.

What happened was right! From happy to sad, from bold to hiding behind an Orange Julius cup. I was stunned.

"Promise me you won't tell anyone back at Gonzaga?" Barb grabbed me by my T-shirt and leaned in an inch from my face.

"No problem."

"I knew I should have been more aggressive finding a husband when I had the chance," she gritted.

Her sour shaking puss snapped into a scary fake smile as a customer bee-lined inside to marvel at the yellow wool coats in their featured position at the store's entrance.

"Aren't those great?" she perked, walking toward the customers like I'd vanished. "They are a must-have, don't you think?"

This was no longer my Barb. An alien had invaded her body. She was unfuckable now.

My dear cousin Barb was my first painful glimpse of "graduate disillusionment." Being manager meant she earned three dollars more than minimum wage. She usually worked the store alone, or while babysitting that gum-smacking teenager who was either there for the 20 percent employee discount or to help her friends shoplift.

But I suspected something else wasn't right. Sure, Barb had hit the skids for now, but I knew her well enough from growing up to know that she must have been porking Chess King Chet for more than his lame paycheck, or for that juicy zit on his left cheek. And I was right. Turns out Chet had just won a national MTV contest, where the one and only Howard Jones would come to the winner's hometown to perform a concert for you and several hundred friends. It was tonight! I couldn't believe it. The stars were already aligning for me, and this was only my first week out of college. Howard could be the first pool I swam in once I got to LA. We could sip expensive cocktails together and bond after tonight's show.

That night, satellite-dished MTV trucks surrounded the biggest country western bar in the county. Looking around at the crowd outside, it seemed like the entire town had shown up for just a glimpse of the star, even if they'd never heard of Howard.

But unless you remotely knew the Chess King (or blew one of the roadies on the MTV truck, like Barb's employee did) you had to be happy standing outside, listening to the vibrations of Howard laboring through his obligatory two hours.

Not us though. Chess King was the VIP, so we got to stand in a special roped off section near the stage that had free pretzels, cut-up celery, and carrot sticks. We were so close up that while Howard was performing that same song that Chet sang at the mall, Chet decided to join in so loudly that Howard had to hold his left ear just to stay in tune.

"Knock it off, man." I hit Chet to stop. He was ruining my chances of being best friends.

"This guy owes me. He got this gig 'cause of me," Chet said, jamming his thumbs into his belt loops to savor his first, last, and only fifteen minutes of fame.

"Ladies and gentlemen! Let's hear it for *Howard Jones!*" the local promoter bellowed like an auctioneer, holding his outstretched arm to Howard. Howard winced and looked to his drummer, clearly pissed he got tricked into this gig.

Before the last song, the promoter invited Chet up on stage for congratulations, making Howard wince again. This was my chance to sneak backstage so Howard could recognize me as the coolest guy in Medford. "Could you believe that asshole?" I practiced saying in the back room, shaking my head, "Let's hang out in LA? El-aye." I said it ten different ways, deciding an emotionless, low-toned version where just my tongue moved sounded the best.

Just then, Howard hurried backstage, ruffling his spiked hair back and forth at his manager. "Let's get the fuck out of this shitbox."

"Hey, Howard?" I said, extending my hand. "Remember me from out there? I was the one that—"

"What?"

Howard looked at me and jerked his thumb backward to the cheering crowd.

"Do your friends call you Howie?" I asked.

"What?"

"I'm blowing this shitbox too. Moving to LA tomorrow."

"Kid." Howard grabbed a black Sharpie pen off a speaker and autographed the left breast of my T-shirt. Dammit. Fuck! I must have said "LA" wrong. He just ruined my best T-shirt. "We've got a lot to break down. It's band members only back here."

"I'm going to be an Alain Michael model," I blurted. As soon as I said it, I knew why I never told anyone. Howard just stared at me, turned, and boarded his bus. I wasn't used to getting the brush-off in my life. It didn't feel good. But I'd better get used to it in the big city. Fuck him. His loss. I had a big day on the road tomorrow anyway.

## Chapter 4

# On the Road, Again

Barb got up early in her cramped one-bedroom apartment and made us scrambled eggs and toast. She wore a pink tank top with no bra and baby blue cotton sweats. Chet insisted on spending the night even after all of her excuses, and was still snoring away in her bedroom. The smell of everyone's sour party breath hung in the air over the burnt toast.

"Did you guys?" I pistoned my index finger in my cylindered other hand.

"Gross. No." He'd have to take me to a hundred Howard concerts for that."

"How are you going to get rid of him?" I almost whispered.

"Wait till he wakes up and then walk around the room and casually show him these." Barb glanced in her bedroom and then lifted her arms up toward me, baring her hairy armpits. "I've been growing them since the day he asked me to Howard."

"What if he's into it?" I laughed.

"Cousin Barb will think of something else. Don't you worry." She walked me out to my Jeep, tucked a few Oregon green buds in my chest pocket and tossed a newly carved pipe made out of a green apple on my front seat.

"This will make the trip go quicker," she said, hugging me tighter than ever, like a mother sending her child off to war. *If she knows something I don't, why doesn't she just tell me?*

The freeway on-ramp conveniently said, "Los Angeles." As if LA was just down the road instead of seven hundred miles away.

I sparked up Barb's gift before the speedometer hit seventy. It soothed my anxiety of the unknown ahead. My mind raced forward about my new life, the people I'd meet, and the right way to act in order to keep up with my cool new friends. Most of all I knew I had to keep my mouth shut and count to ten before I let whatever was on my mind rip.

"Honey, everybody thinks those things. They just don't say them," Mom used to correct me. Mom called my little problem "social Tourette's." But blurting out things always made me feel better, like letting out a fart instead of holding it in. And at least I could be honest.

The grass on the side of the freeway was gradually changing from green to gold. I was getting pretty bored. Near Sacramento I started to yawn every two minutes, so I reached into the glove box and chewed up four No-Doz tablets that were left over from finals week. They worked pretty well until about an hour past Stockton, where even the ammonia smells of cow manure around the feeding lots weren't doing the trick.

*Alain is expecting me!* I reminded myself to keep me going. I promised him I would be there tonight, and I had better be on time to show him I was reliable and properly excited about this rare opportunity he was offering me. At first I wasn't excited about this gig at Alain's, but if things worked out, this could be amazing.

I pulled to the shoulder to pee in a ditch and decided to chop up the remaining No-Doz with my key. I snorted it right there on the dashboard. Unlike cocaine, which I swear to you I've only done three times, it tasted like delicious peppermint. It even thumped my heart in the same way, leaving me to wonder why the manufacturers didn't suggest this alternative method on the box.

# Chapter 5

# El Aye

Cruising down the big hill of the 405 Freeway past Mulholland Drive, I looked to my left at a man-made creek that looked like the water was flowing uphill. Straight ahead, a glowing moving ribbon of yellowish white and twinkling red stretched out as far as the horizon. Traffic was beautiful. It made me almost forget the last ten ass-wrenching hours. Right here on the freeway in front of me were more cars than in all of Spokane County. It was exciting to be a part of such a mass of humanity. Until it all came to a screeching halt. Couldn't these fucking people just drive! This stop and go was making my clutch stink, and if that burned out, I'd be sunk.

"Hey cutie! you new to town?" yelled a brunette beauty of unknown age from her silver convertible Mercedes. She was dressed in a skimpy tennis outfit. A full-grown woman hitting on me? This was a first. I was too shocked to answer. All I could do was smile.

She ignored the honks from an angry man behind her while she wrote her phone number on the rubber line of a tennis ball.

"Catch!" she screamed, tossing it toward me. I caught it, held it up, kissed the ball and smiled some more. Janice. Huh. LA and I were going to get along just fine. It was never this easy in Spokane.

I exited at Sunset Boulevard and followed Alain's directions, driving past lawns as smooth as Mrs. P's until I arrived at an iron-gated house on Amalfi Street. I pressed the brass buzzer. The gate slowly opened and Alain's girlfriend appeared, wearing the same pink T-shirt.

"Hey."

"It's Lauren," she snapped, sounding like a bitch. *Whoa crazy daisy? Like I am supposed to remember your name? Shit.* I always forget names.

"Park behind the hydrangeas." She pointed behind the garage.

"Alain won't like looking at this." She splayed her hands at my Jeep.

"And I don't know where you are going to put all this stuff." She thwacked a bungee cord just like Mrs. P, making my heart sink.

"Your room is small, and Alain doesn't get back until tomorrow."

"That's okay. Looks like a pretty good neighborhood to me," I said, stretching my arms overhead, trying to lighten her mood.

Lauren didn't smile back, making me think my whole trip down here might have been a big mistake.

"Do you have something to wear besides that?" she asked.

"Sure. These are just my ordinary clothes."

"Because there's a party tonight, and Alain wants you to go."

Truth was most of my clothes looked the same. My mainstay was blue jeans and white T-shirts, though now I was down to one good T-shirt after Howard ruined my best one. I could at least find her something that smelled better. Maybe I would wear the T-shirt that had a breast pocket to dress things up a bit.

Lauren walked me through the side door near the garage to my single bed jammed near the washer and dryer.

"Hope this is okay."

I had slept in much, much worse. Just beyond the open Mr. Ed door, a lit-up pool glistened against the early evening glow of orange and blue sky.

"Where do you and Alain sleep?"

She scrunched her face. "We're not together. Alain is…"

She softened a bit, like she had some compassion for me.

"Alain is what?"

"Between relationships. I'm just his assistant."

I walked through the well-kept ranch house, past the slated entryway and vaulted beamed ceiling to the other side of the house, where Lauren mentioned two guys just like me were staying. I was anxious to meet them and find out more of what I could expect and hurried over to their room. I leaned against the door for what seemed like fifteen minutes.

One guy was at the mirror making model faces and blow drying his hair. The other one was playing Atari video games with headphones on. Suddenly Lauren barged past me.

"Sean, the driver will be here in thirty minutes! You're not even ready."

"I am," I said.

"Who's he?" Sean, the one at the mirror, scowled.

"Uggh. Jack. I told you, you can't wear that. Sean, loan him that new shirt Alain bought you."

"No. Goddammit, Lauren. I *earned* it. I haven't even had a chance to wear it!" Sean screamed, turning off his hair dryer and banging it twice on the counter to make his point.

"Look, don't you 'goddammit' me. We'll ship you back to Garden Grove so fast."

"He really should wear it first," I pleaded.

"Marcus, turn that shit off; it's going to make you more boring than you already are." Lauren marched over and flipped the headphones off Marcus's head on her way to grabbing a pink satin shirt from the closet. "Wear it, or I'll tell Alain." She thrust the shirt in my hands.

Wearing the stupid thing two sizes too small was the least I could do. Based on the house alone, this was quite an opportunity they were giving me. Thank God those striped pants of Sean's didn't fit me, or Sean would have hated me even more.

A white stretch limo was waiting for us in the driveway. The last time I was in a limo I was drunk and shirtless after high school prom. It might sound like it was a great night, but it didn't end up that way. It was right up there as a contender for the worst day of my life. After prom, we had just dropped off my buddy Tom and his girlfriend up on the south hill and were headed back down Grand Boulevard to the north side. My girlfriend, Lindsey, and two good friends were taking turns standing up through the sunroof, hooting and a hollering. I was taking a breather sitting backward near the front Plexiglas divider.

The accident happened just in front of Manito Park. An eight-point buck ran out in front of the limo. Yes, a fucking deer, in the middle of the city. The driver swerved to avoid it, hit the curb, and slammed the limo head-on into a maple tree. I whammed the back of my head on the Plexiglas. It hurt like hell, but no big deal. My two good friends, and my prom date, Lindsey, my first real girlfriend ever, were not so lucky. You know how they tell you not to stand up out of the sunroof in a limo? And you think they are just being a buzz kill? Well, I can tell you why. When we hit the tree, Lindsey and my best friend, Carl, slammed their heads on the hood of the car so hard they were knocked out cold. My other buddy, Henry, did some kind of flip somersault out of the roof and tried to walk it off. He kept holding his stomach and trying to make jokes while I tried to get him to sit down and wait until help arrived. Then he lay down.

"I can't breathe; I can't breathe," Henry kept saying over and over. "I'm sorry, man."

It didn't make any sense why he was apologizing to me, but I tried to calm him down and tend to everyone at the same time. It was hell. Then the neighbor guy came out in his white bathrobe yelling about his tree until he saw how serious everything was and ran inside to call for help. The driver's face was pretty banged up. I am still furious at the driver to this day. He seemed mad at us for getting hurt, like he was going to be in even more trouble than he already was for crashing the limo.

Everyone died that night except for me and the driver—internal bleeding, all of them. After all the funerals, I felt guilty to be alive—until my buddy Tom told me Henry and Lindsey were screwing around behind my back. I wish he had never told me. He said he was trying to help me get over everything quicker, but hearing that didn't take any of the pain of their death away. It just made me a little more cynical about life and love and made it harder for me to trust.

So that's why on this limo ride tonight, I chose to sit up front with the driver. Lauren, Sean, and Marcus were so busy looking at themselves in back they didn't even miss me until we arrived at another gated driveway, fashionably late, for some action movie premiere party filled with well-dressed people with open-collared shirts hugging each other like they were all best friends.

"Why are we here?" I asked Sean as we were admitted through the foyer amid flashing cameras.

"Look around, smarty farm boy. This is how business gets done. You better not spill anything on that shirt."

I guess I could hug randoms if it meant being cast in their movie. I tried to stretch the way-too-tight shirt to ease my breath by gently grabbing either shoulder until I heard a rrrrrrip. Sean darted a look down at his prized shirt, wondering if he had heard the sound correctly.

"Don't stand next to me. This is my area," Sean insisted, drawing an imaginary three-foot radius around himself.

I drifted over to the shrimp tray, past where Marcus stood gaping toward the bushes. He looked so boring I didn't dare get too close to him for fear he'd snatch part of my brain. I started wolfing down those beautiful shrimp two at a time, sometimes slowing down enough to scoop up the cocktail sauce, but those babies were just as delicious plain. I had never seen so many shrimp in my life. After I got about fifteen of them in me, I realized I hadn't eaten since just before I snorted the No Doz.

"And who might you be?" a very tanned fifty-year-old woman with pink lips and super white eyes asked me. I hugged her and swallowed my mouthful of shrimp, wondering where I could wipe my slimy hands. I opted for the back of her shirt.

"Jack Fitzpatrick." I offered my cleanish hand to show her I was more than just a good hugger.

Sean swooped out of the shadows and turned the woman toward him. "Louise, you look great! You did such an amazing job on that After School Special." He hugged her.

Lauren swaggered up. "I can see you've met the newest addition to Alain's dream team. Isn't he delicious?" Lauren said, sounding a little bit like Cher. I liked it when Lauren kissed my ass like this. Maybe she was just giving me tough love earlier at the house.

I shouldered Sean out of the way to give Louise an even more professional handshake this time, but she just hugged me again.

"Mmmm. We'll be in touch, Lauren," Louise purred, patting me on the butt.

Lauren nodded in approval as Louise walked away.

"You did fine, Jack. But next time, during the hug with potentials, don't pull back on your pelvic region," Lauren said, thrusting her warm vagina directly on my thigh like she wanted a horsy ride. "Get it?" She looked me in the eye to make sure I understood.

She was no longer sexy. At all. She was like a creepy high school teacher just past her prime who kept figuring out ways for her male students to stare at her cleavage.

The next morning, Alain arrived home from his trip in a dark, sour mood and wouldn't speak to anyone except Lauren.

"Porker!" he said. "They called me a porker! Can you believe it?" He waved the latest *National Enquirer* like it was on fire. Lauren kept her eyes down and robotically wiped the same spot on the counter top over and over like a Stepford wife.

"Carrots and poached fish—that's all we're eating. I can't do this alone, Lauren." Alain drifted to the living room in a daze.

"Did you ask him where I could put my stuff?" I chimed at Lauren.

Lauren put one finger over her lips and beckoned me to follow her down the hall to the TV room, where she popped in a Jane Fonda exercise video. My punishment for my question.

"Do it. Alain's orders." She kept one hand on the door jamb and roared down the hall, "Sean! Get in here!"

Sean had to be better than me at the video, too.

"You've got to kick higher! Point your toes. Like her!" Sean pointed at Jane on the screen. Sean's moves, tight shorts, and headband made him the spitting image of Jane Fonda with a dick.

Marcus, the boring guy playing video games from the first night, was sent home this morning while I was still sleeping, so I did it—at least when Lauren was in the room. Sean said the reason that Marcus got booted was that he didn't hug anyone at the party.

# Chapter 6

# Getting Lighter

I woke up starving the next morning and found Lauren in the kitchen nibbling a plain rice cake with both hands like a mouse with cheese. Rice cakes were awful, a crunchy way to capture air and eat it. They were only remotely palatable if you slathered them in something bad for you, like peanut butter, and then what was the point?

"I have to go to the drugstore." I lied. I was starving. I needed something like a burger. Anything. Food that would stick to my ribs and get rid of that ticking hunger that started in my stomach and traveled all the way up to my right ear.

"For what?" she insisted, with one hand on her hip. "Alain doesn't like his people leaving, except to go on go-sees."

"Go-sees?"

"You know, like go see if you'll get the job. And if you think you are going to eat something while you are out, think again. You'll be outta here."

"Lauren, I ..." I stalled, trying to think up a believable lie.

"What is it? You know you can tell me anything."

"I have this rash," I pointed to my crotch. This was my variation of the tearful "I had my period in my white pants" excuse that I learned from my high school girlfriend after we got caught for skipping. I got six hours of detention, but all she did was wear a skirt and look shy around the principal for a week.

"Where is it?" she asked.

"Well, you know, around my thing."

"Can I see it?"

I might have been able to throw up on her at that point when I imagined doing that for her, but I had no food in my stomach.

"Well, I suppose you can go to the drugstore then," she said, realizing she was being creepy. "But can you pick me up some Campho Phenique, sweetie?" She pointed to a new canker sore the size of an unbroken Ruffle potato chip on her lip. Eww. That wasn't there last night, or I wouldn't have let her give me her hugging lessons.

"Sure." I guess the sweetie part meant I had to pay for it.

I took a nice long drive in the Jeep down La Cienega Boulevard and searched for the familiar cheap calories I knew so well back home. I knew I was getting close when all the buildings began to look like they needed a paint job. I stopped at a place called Juicyburger and parked the Jeep past the five-car-deep drive-through line so I could keep an eye on my stuff. It was always quicker to go inside rather than wait in the drive-through, unless you were the only one in line.

I sat down at an anchored orange table with my tray piled high: triple cheeseburger, chili fries, and a large real Coke. Next to me sat a fat kid whose mom stuck her palm in front of his face so he would stop staring at my tray.

"Want some?" I asked. The kid clearly wanted seconds.

He nodded.

"Don't take calories from strangers, Billy," she huffed. She grabbed her Weeble by the hand and stood up, looking back to dart one last angry look at me.

*Take Billy to a salad bar, bitch.* I couldn't be bothered to care about anyone. I was in fast-food heaven: grease, ketchup, mayonnaise, and salt. Nothing fought too hard on its way down, soothing my fear of this new, colorful life cruising by in large cars low to the ground.

I was watching the traffic when terror struck. Shit! It was Alain! Right there! Pulling into the fucking drive-through line in his baby blue BMW convertible! There was nowhere to hide. He'd recognize my shit-filled Jeep for sure. If I didn't sneak out now, he'd send me packing back to Spokane!

I threw down the last precious burger bite, that morsel as prized as the center of a cinnamon roll, and ran out under the angry glares of a table of after-church-goers, clearly upset I hadn't cleared my table. I knew all about fast-food protocol, but this was an emergency. I ran toward my Jeep. Billy and his bitchy mom were parked right next to me.

"You promised me a milkshake!" Billy screamed, blocking my driver side, splaying his arms and legs out so wide that his mom couldn't hoist him into their minivan.

"You again!" she sneered.

"Get him in there like a Christmas tree," I said. "Head first." I lifted Billy up by his belt loop and tossed him in, closing their sliding door.

I hopped in my Jeep and gunned it onto La Cienega without looking, narrowly beating a band of cars speeding toward me after their green light. I glanced back and saw Alain just turning the corner to the pickup window. All this bullshit had better be worth it. But something didn't feel right. I felt free. Lighter. I looked in my rearview mirror. I *was* lighter.

"Fuck!" I pulled over and scanned the Jeep. I'd been ripped off. Everything. They even took Janice's tennis ball. The Jeep had never been this barren. This was all Lauren's fault. She could have easily found a corner of the garage for me to use, and none of this would have happened. That cold sore could eat her face now for all I cared.

I skidded into Alain's driveway, easily beating him home. I sulked around the side of the house and went in through my private door to lie down on my single bed with my shoes still on. I seethed at the ceiling until I heard Alain drive up. Lauren ran outside like an obedient dog.

"How was your workout, babe? You're still sweating."

I marched out to join them. These two were finally going to get a piece of my mind.

"I just can't seem to lose this." Alain grabbed his Buddha belly and thrust it at Lauren before glancing at me for some sympathy.

"You got a little something here," I said, pointing at an eraser-sized glop of ketchup that had taken up residence between his eyebrows. He looked like a pudgy Indian woman with an edible beauty spot. He must have really made love to his triple burger for the ketchup to reach up that high. And I bet that asshole got to eat the last bite, too.

"Has Louise Rosenthal called back about Jack?" Alain said to distract Lauren, wiping his forehead and blushing as red as the ketchup before licking his finger after he realized he couldn't wipe it on his pants.

"No, not yet. He's got four go-sees tomorrow and six on Friday."

"Good, good."

Of course, she had told me nothing, and it probably wasn't even true.

"Is Lauren taking good care of you?" Alain patted my shoulder.

"Like a prince," I said. Lauren seemed pleased that I lied. I was catching on.

"Consuela said lunch is almost ready." Lauren offered.

"Oh, good. I haven't eaten all day." Alain rubbed his hands together, making Lauren squeal and make baby claps because she made him happy.

"Me neither." I winked at Lauren, who stopped her acting to touch her cold sore. Let her wonder. I was still pissed but thought it might be smarter to throw a fit *after* lunch, so I could storm off to my room in a dramatic exit if I needed to.

In the week I'd been there, Consuela always dressed in a yellow simple dress with a white apron and white shoes. Her real name was Maria, but since Alain started calling her Consuela the first day, she never corrected him. She never said much to any of us, and when she did it was in minimal broken English, even though I'd heard her speak on the phone with barely an accent when she thought no one was around.

Consuela set the lunch table with a clean white tablecloth near the pool, under the largest palm tree for shade. This part of my new life was amazing. Her poached fish and vegetables actually tasted pretty great, but during lunch, Sean kept interrupting me whenever I tried to say something. So I started opening my mouth and just pretending to speak. He never caught on. It was kind of fun to watch him talk about nothing and bore the hell out of Alain and Lauren. Plus I got to eat his seconds.

Afterward, I was too stuffed to fight. I lay down on my bed, grabbed the phone on the nightstand, and called up Mom to lie to her about how everything was going great in my new cushy office job I'd invented for myself.

"Mrs. Pohlkiss asked how you were doing." Mom smiled over the phone.

"What did you say?" I sat up.

"Just what you'd want me to." Mom laughed. "I told her you'd already gotten a promotion."

"It's good to hear you lightening up, Mom." She knew all about my relationship with Mrs. P.

"I'm just glad I don't have to worry about you anymore," she said.

Wow. That felt good. I hung up even more motivated to make this model/movie star thing work. In a few short months, I might be in a commercial or maybe even a movie. I didn't care which, but Mrs. Pohlkiss would shit her drawers if either happened.

After a couple good farts, I jumped out of bed and hurried over to Sean's room. I was so amped and motivated now I was curious to know if even *he* could kill my happy buzz. I plopped down on the couch and joined him watching TV.

"Da plane. Da plane!" He pointed to Tatu on *Fantasy Island* and then clicked the remote several more times to find another channel.

"Whatchu talking 'bout, Willis," he said pouting his lips in his version of a black accent. It was a time like this that I missed Charles. If Sean was him I could just sit on his face and fart away his annoying behavior, but knowing Sean, he would run screaming to Lauren or Alain and try to get me kicked out to lessen the competition.

"You're really good at those voices," I said without the slightest bit of sarcasm.

"Yeah, I know," he said, clicking the remote to the next show.

Lauren stood at the doorway.

"Jack, did you get my product?"

"No. Sorry. I was itching so bad I forgot."

"Then, Sean, it looks like you get Jack's appointments tomorrow." Lauren turned her palms to the sky to signal, "That's that."

Sean slyed his eyes at me.

"Thank you, sweetie," Sean said.

I was furious, but there was no way I would give either of them the satisfaction of my disappointment.

"Looks like I get the day off, then." I smiled and cocked my head. Lauren was no match for Mrs. Pohlkiss. I jumped up.

"Where do you think you're going?" Lauren held her arm outstretched against my chest.

"For a run. Gotta stay in shape! Remember?" I took her arm away and kissed her hand.

I reached down and double-slapped the quad of Sean's spaghetti noodle leg.

"Lauren!" he whined, smoothing his long bangs behind his ear with one hand and rubbing his leg with the other. "Can Alain buy me another shirt? That pink one smells like Jack now."

"No. And, Jack, don't be long," Lauren said, even more annoyed now that she wasn't the boss of me.

Exercise was essential when someone fucked me over like this. I could focus all my anger to make me run faster or lift more weights. Usually by the end of the workout, I wasn't as pissed anymore. It worked for ten years with Mrs. P. I don't know how Mom put up with her. Maybe she took it out on the floors she scrubbed. I remember one time Mom was on her hands and knees while Mrs. P stood over her, pointing out dirt spots she'd missed with her foot.

In my room, I searched through my duffel filled with what was left of my clothes. I didn't have an extra T-shirt to spare, so I set off running in just my red surf shorts toward the beach. I ran at least five miles until I found the Jonathan Club, a private club right on the sand. It didn't even have tennis courts; it was just a place for people to mingle without the riffraff. I stopped to watch the members laughing and feeling special about their lives while they gazed out at the ocean, dining on beautiful burgers stacked high with red onion and avocado, and plates loaded with so many french fries that a normal person couldn't eat them all. But I could. I wanted to be part of this club-sooner than later. I even scanned the crowd for Janice, the tennis ball lady. There were plenty here that looked just like her.

That night after my big run I ate carrots and apples alone in my room. That's all there was in the fridge. There was no point in hanging out with Sean. It was like teasing a dumb dog that you knew was never going to be your friend. A dog you'd consider throwing a stick off a cliff-for him to go fetch. The kind of dog you shouldn't bring to the pound, since whatever poor kid who adopted it next would have to go through the same shit.

I tapped off the light and decided to jack off to Janice, and to what she might have taught me. After prom night, I really didn't go out with many girls in college. Because when I started to like them, it made me think of my dead ex-girlfriend, and everything that went down. Plus, at Gonzaga, the really good girls that I *did* want to be with were way too much work to get into their pants. And if I did try, maybe after all that work, I'd just get screwed over again, and I couldn't take that. I kept my snogging limited to late-night, drunken stuff after parties, where I'd never see the girl again.

After I finished my beat-off-bank session with Janice, I wiped up with one of my socks and drifted off to sleep, completely relaxed and happy that at the very least I had made it this far from Spokane and was living in a Beverly Hills mansion, sort of. Even with all the bad stuff, things were pretty good. I could buy more cheap clothes with my first paycheck.

In my dream, Janice was lying behind me, telling me how much I turned her on, giving me a reach-around. I felt her beautiful large breasts pressing against my back. Her hairy chest tickled my shoulder blades. Wait! What the fuck?! I jumped out of bed, nearly breaking the overhead light.

"Come on back," a voice from the dark beckoned. I stumbled to the wall and felt for the light switch. A hairy mass of flesh was on my bed, a sheet draped over one of its legs.

"Turn that off!" Alain blocked his eyes.

I looked down at the open flap of my green-striped boxers and closed it.

"How long have you been here?" I demanded.

"I'm just helping you sleep."

"I was sleeping just fine, dickhead."

"You don't want Sean to get all the jobs, do you?" he asked, patting the spot on the bed next to him, making his man boobs jiggle.

"I fucking knew it! Fuck!" I started to shove what was left of my stuff in my duffel.

"What are you doing?"

"I'm getting the fuck out of here."

"You didn't think you could just live here rent free did you, country boy?"

"Eat shit, man boobs!"

I hurled my sock smeared with half of Janice's and my offspring at his head. He batted it away. If he knew I just cleaned up with it, I'm sure he would have kept it.

"Calm down. It's just two men being men. I didn't mean the country boy thing."

I shook my head and continued packing as fast as I could. Alain stood up.

"You've got nowhere to go. LA is a dangerous place. There are a lot of creepy people out there."

"I know." I cocked my fist and punched him in the arm as hard as I could instead of his face.

Alain rubbed his arm and started to cry. It was a fake cry, like a spoiled kid crying to his mother for another piece of cake.

"You're not fucking worth a punch in the face," I said.

Alain pouted. "Do you do this with everyone who stays here?" I asked.

"Only if they're cute."

"You and Sean?"

"Only a few times. You and I could be exclusive, if you want." He said eagerly.

"Exclusively what?"

"You could have your own apartment."

"With you in it? No, thanks."

"It would be all yours. Please don't leave."

I was almost finished packing.

"Look, I don't even have to touch you." Alain pleaded.

I sat down on the bed and stopped packing and left the duffle zipper open. I began to calm down and wonder if I was making the biggest mistake of my life.

"That's right," he soothed.

"Seriously?" I took a deep breath. "Okay. Cool."

"Good." Alain wiped his acting tears, smearing his mascara. "You can stand all the way over there."

"What? Why?" I looked toward where he pointed, and moved in that direction.

"You can just jerk off for me."

That was it! I couldn't do it. I smashed my bare foot against Alain's chest, knocking him flat on the bed. I stormed outside to my Jeep in my boxers into the cool night air, hurling my duffle into the backseat.

"I won't even take pictures. This time," Alain yelled after me.

I tore out of Alain's driveway and drove in second gear to give myself time to think. I opened my wallet. After gas and whatnot, I was down to $359. That would be gone after three nights in a Holiday Inn. I thought about turning around and going back inside. I could put off Alain for a few more days until maybe I could get some work, but I just couldn't do it. No matter what, he'd be in control of my work, and of me, and if that happened, that would be something I couldn't wash off in the shower at night. In the hidden pocket of my wallet, underneath the credit card holder slits that held no credit cards, was the address of my best buddy, Dexter, in Newport Beach. Dexter was my only chance.

I pulled onto the 405, headed south. It was two in the morning, and the freeway was thick with traffic—a rush hour filled with happy drunks fresh off last call. Everyone was happy, except for me.

Mrs. Pohlkiss and Alain were right. A boy like me had no business here in the big city. At least it wasn't raining. But then it started. First, just one drop. I looked up. Did a bird pee on me? Then a deluge of drops, like November in Spokane. Mom was right. I should have brought my hardtop just in case. In the glow of lights I pictured Sean and Alain in bed with the sheets pulled up to their chins, laughing at me. I pulled over and cried until I lost track of time.

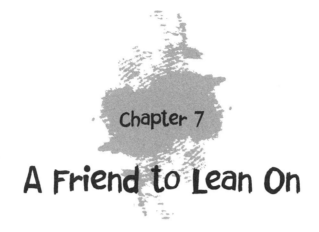

# Chapter 7

# A Friend to Lean On

The windshields headed east on the Newport Beach freeway glowed deep orange from the rising sun. My cry fest hadn't lasted long enough. It was still too early to wake Dexter.

Dexter didn't care if I failed. We had failed together plenty of times as dorm mates freshman year. At first, I didn't know what to make of him, driving a brand new 1983 black Trans Am with a gold bird on the hood. A free car is a free car, I hear that, but I had to speak up and draw the line when he unpacked his drawer full of colored bikini underwear. Apparently that's what they wear down under, down under in South Africa, but that wasn't going to fly here. This guy needed my help.

Dexter found Gonzaga by accident after he and his mom packed up everything and moved to America for a fresh start after *his* dad died. He didn't talk about it much, but what little he did tell me, about this thing called apartheid, was that some native South Africans broke into their ranch when Dex and his mom were gone, and ended up putting a tire around his dad's neck and burning him alive. Right then, I was glad I didn't know the details of my dad's death.

Dexter thought he got accepted to Georgetown because we have the same school colors and mascot, and we were both in a place called Washington. But no. Gonzaga was the only school that accepted him.

You gotta love Dexter's mom. She not only wanted her son to fit in, she wanted him to be cool in his new country. That's why she bought him the Trans Am. *Smokey and the Bandit* had just become a hit in South Africa, seven years late, just before they moved.

I remember riding with Dexter one night on the way to get the twenty-five-cent pitchers for college night at the Black Dog in Idaho, since the drinking age was only nineteen. While we waited at a stoplight, Dexter pointed over to a mirror-sunglassed guy beside us, sporting a full-length mullet. His leather driving gloves gripped the wheel of an identical Trans Am to Dexter's.

"Why is that guy revving his engine and looking at us?" Dexter asked.

"Because you guys are like brothers," I said. Dexter scrunched his face and looked down at his car, and then at the man's.

"But I have leather seats, and a premium sound system and—"

"Still brothers."

Soon after that, the Trans-Am sunroof t-tops went permanently missing after being used as snow sleds at Indian Canyon golf course. The gold bird on the hood was obliterated with a cut-out of Angus Young wailing on guitar, and a blown up rubber was tied to the bent antenna as a wind sock. With just those small adjustments, Dexter had officially reached campuswide cooldom within a week.

Just like back on the south hill, I pulled into the lookout at the top of Newport bluff and gazed out from my Jeep at the miniature mansions dotting the pristine sand islands. Yachts were moored in their front yards by the sparkling emerald grout of the bay. Bloody Dexter. It would be great to see him again. This was the place!

I drove down the small hill past Hoag Hospital and parallel parked into the first spot I could find near the beach. I closed my eyes, refusing to think about what happened with Alain and drifted off. The beep beep beeping of a street sweeper woke me some time later. I wiped the drool from the side of my mouth. I must have been out for at least an hour.

The boardwalk stirred with yummy mummies holding paper coffee cups, pushing strollers with large wheels that looked sturdy enough to be towed behind my Jeep going 70 mph. The moms in Spokane didn't have fancy strollers like these, and they didn't walk around holding a coffee cup to their lips like a pacifier.

On the beach, surfers in neon wetsuits looked extra cool, running, instead of walking, to the waves, with their boards tucked under their arms. For the first time in my life, it seemed like no one noticed me. I was homeless. It was time to go to Dexter's and change that.

I walked into Lucky's grocery store, grabbed three bananas, and approached the almost-grandma cashier.

"Eight-nine cents, please."

"Can you tell me where Linda Isle is?"

"You're going to Linda Isle, and all you're bringing is three bananas?" She smiled.

"I'm going to eat them right now. They're getting nothing from me." I smiled back.

"Just over that little bridge there."

I could have walked. I drove over the bridge and was surprised how small the houses were, considering all the Mercedeses parked on the street. Also, there were no front yards. The houses were six feet from each other.

I easily found Dexter's house, a white stucco modern home, took a deep breath, and prayed he would be home. I knocked. Dexter cracked open his front door, sporting his perpetual bed head.

"Well, look what the cat dragged in," Dexter said.

The strain of the past week drained from my body just by seeing his face.

"How the hell did you find me?"

"Honey, who is it?" Mrs. Manchester said in a wonderful thick South African accent. She crowded in behind Dexter and wiped a mixing bowl with her apron. She didn't look much different than the cashier at Lucky's, except for her blue sapphire bracelet and ring.

"Mom, meet Jack, my best friend from college."

"What a nice Sunday surprise!" Mrs. Manchester pulled me into the house. "I've heard so much about you. You were the boy who saved Dexter when he got carjacked."

Carjacking? Dexter was brilliant.

"That's right, I was, wasn't I?" I said.

"Can you stay for breakfast?" She put her arm around my shoulder and moved me toward the kitchen.

"Yeah, I can stay for a lot of them." I winked at Dexter on my way past him, just so he knew who would become the new no. 1 son.

"What brings you to these parts?" she asked.

"Oh. A job."

"Well, your friend Dexter needs to be getting one of those, too. Don't you, honey."

I stared at the view of Newport Bay that filled their floor-to-ceiling windows. White yachts and white sailboats were everywhere, something I'd only seen in pictures, and here it was in front of me. I sank onto a very clean white couch that would have been destroyed in one day if we were back at school. I didn't have the guts to tell Dexter the truth about Alain, and maybe I never would.

"Mine didn't pan out," I said, turning on my dejected puppy look.

"Oh dear." She came over to pat my back. It was just what I needed.

After I explained to her how I got robbed down to my floor mats, she showed me a twin bed in Dexter's room and insisted I stay with them until I got on my feet. Happy days were here again!

"You'll be good motivation for Dexter."

Dexter rolled his eyes. Together we knew we were a parent's worst nightmare.

The following month could only be described as utter twenty-one-year-old bliss: daily drinking and sexing up perfectly toned babes that we'd meet on the beach in front of Dexter's house every day. Unlike Gonzaga girls, these girls didn't have as much beef, and usually got drunk on two beers 'cause they were so thin. On weekends, somebody would know somebody whose parents were gone and had a fabulous house with a view every bit as good as what we had, and we'd party till dawn;-only to awaken in fresh sheets sometime in the early afternoon to a well-stocked fridge, complete with milk in a glass quart bottle and expensive deli meats and cheeses, with names such as Camembert, and other stuff that tasted amazing on toast under the broiler when we were hammered. Mrs. Manchester had a charge account at a fancier store that was near Lucky's called Gelson's. It looked like they shined up each grape on display. Almost every day we made sure the fridge was stocked. It gave us something to do, and we didn't want to disappoint Mrs. Manchester in case she got the munchies too.

I was living an NC-17 movie with no plot. But things started to turn a little sour around the fifth week, after Mrs. Manchester got the latest bill from Gelson's. I caught a glance at it. It was almost as much as a semester at Gonzaga. That's when her cheerful glances toward me became much less frequent, and the conversations I'd drum up with her started to sound like ass-kissing. But the final blow was when something happened to her white Haitian cotton couch.

It was the one pristine thing she had in her house—something she could always control and count on. I loved it too, for the soothing way it hugged my bottom just right, and the coolness and sheen of its expensive fabric on my bare forearm.

I didn't put my shoes on it or anything. I knew better than to even sit on it when she was around, always opting for the floor or a kitchen chair instead. The incident happened during what Dexter and I referred to as "love in the afternoon." Normally, like I said, we went to the beach to scope out what might be in store for the evening, but on Wednesdays, Mrs. Manchester had her ceramic painting class. She was gone from noon to four, so that was our time to invite over our chosen favorite girl for daytime exploration. Dexter already had his fun last week, so now it was my turn.

Shelly showed up at twelve thirty on the dot, cute as hell. She had brown, sun-streaked, shiny hair and flawless tanned skin with just a few freckles on her nose. Her body was so perfect she was allowed to wear just a bikini top and short shorts. I had a couple imports chilling for us in the freezer, and even put out some deli meats on a plate, which, by the way, makes it look *way* more sophisticated than just a sandwich. But we didn't need either. By the time the clock on the VCR flashed 12:39, we were both completely naked, rolling around on that forbidden soft couch—its cushions as white and fresh as new-laundered baby diapers.

I was in heaven, except for the fact I needed to take a shit. I could practically hear my mom saying over my shoulder, "Honey, you should have gone earlier." Suddenly I had to go now, and fast.

"I'll be right back," I said, bobbing full mast to the bathroom.

"Hurry up, Jack!" Shelly moaned from the couch.

Explaining to her I was taking a growler would definitely kill the mood, so I turned on the faucet and grimaced like an Olympic weight lifter until success splashed down, like a vintage spaceship without a parachute, into its porcelain ocean.

I rushed out, and moments later we were back twisting and contorting over every inch of the couch. It wasn't until I heard the key in the door that I noticed the skid marks covering the cushions like charcoal on a sketchpad. Another reminder in life: no matter how careful you are, a stray dingleberry can ruin your day.

We somersaulted behind the couch. I tried my best telekinesis. *Please go to your bedroom, please. Go take a shit. Something. Just don't come in here.*

"I got all the way out there, and class was canceled," Mrs. Manchester announced, her high heels clicking toward us like a predator's talons on the tile.

"Dexter?"

I peeked around the back side of the couch. Mrs. Manchester spotted our clothes first. She reached down to pick them up and gasped when she found Shelly's swim top. Then a blood-curdling scream. It was the couch. Mrs. Manchester dropped to her knees and pored over the brown strokes of my unplanned art project with her manicured fingers and then with her nose. I wanted to stop Mrs. Manchester, but I was paralyzed by the fear of being sent home. Suddenly I was back at the Pohlkiss's front lawn, watching Mrs. P sniff Montana's "M."

"Hi," I said.

Mrs. Manchester slowly peered over the couch. I rolled on top of Shelly.

"Back so soon?" I asked.

Mrs. M put her hands on her hips, cocked her head to the side and said nothing. She walked away, each tap of her heels sounding like a nail in my coffin marked SPOKANE, COD.

"That's so gross!" Shelly laughed, holding her stomach, looking at the skid marks.

I sat naked on the carpet, Indian style, looking down to my upward palms resting in my lap in disbelief.

Shelly grabbed her things. "You're still cute, pookie. Call me." She slinked out the alley side door to the beach with her clothes in hand, wearing just her shorts.

I slid on my boxers and ran to the kitchen sink cabinet for the spot remover. As I began scrubbing the marks, I realized the virgin couch and my relationship with Mrs. Manchester were never going to be the same.

Mrs. Manchester approached me where I knelt by the couch.

"I'm," I gulped.

"There's no need to be sorry."

"I really—"

"I just don't think you should be exposing Dexter to this kind of behavior."

I nodded. She was in complete denial that her son was a whore.

"And if you had your own place …" She walked to the kitchen without finishing her sentence. She made herself a sandwich without asking *me* if I wanted one while I continued to scrub. This was bad. She had never done that before. She was through with me. I was a sinner.

"Please don't mention this," she insisted. "He doesn't need to be getting any ideas." I nodded and scrubbed till the clean spots were whiter than the rest of the couch. It looked terrible now, like my neighbor back in Hillyard who used to frost and tip her own hair and then do yard work while wearing the skullcap like it was something everybody should do.

An hour later, Dexter slammed the front door and headed back to our room. Our little secret I was keeping lasted four minutes. Dexter laughed so hard I had to turn up the music to drown out his honking. Mrs. Manchester poked her head in to see what the commotion was. She wasn't stupid. I was busted. Now I felt worse than being caught naked with Shelley.

"Need something, Mom?"

He was picking sides now. Mrs. Manchester closed the door.

"Dude, we have to do something nice for your mom to make it better," I pleaded.

"Fuck that; just pretend nothing happened," he said.

That left us no option but to hit the town hard that night to soothe my guilt and to figure out where I might land next.

The next morning, she stormed into our dark cave and snapped open the roll shades, ranting in an undecipherable accent. Her days as the cheery homemaker were officially over now.

Dexter covered his head with a pillow as she continued raving. Dexter, as her son, was the only one allowed to ignore her. I glanced at the clock. My God! It was ten fifteen in the morning, just past the middle of our night! She must be really mad.

All my concentration was focused on blocking the painful sunlight, so I think I was understandably scared when she lurched in my face and started in on me, sounding like the *wa-wa-wa* of Charlie Brown's teacher.

"Are you stupid?" she asked me, our foreheads an inch apart.

My relief at finally understanding a word she said, coupled with the stress of being interrogated so early, forced a burning hot party fart out of me. Her expression snapped from anger to horror. Then Dexter's pillow broadsided my temple. I used it as a mask to avoid burning my own nose hairs with the stench.

The fart was so bad I couldn't even take a proper breath to tell her how sorry I was. She backed up with both hands against the striped wallpaper, burying her chin in her chest. I knew right then, for sure, I would have to find my own place. But I needed a job first.

## Chapter 8

# Get a Job

As far as job prospects, movie star was out for now. Like I said, I really just wanted to make a lot of money. Enough money so I wouldn't have to listen to anybody's shit. Enough money to show Mrs. P what kind of royalty she fucked with.

I needed a job like Mrs. P's neighbor, the stockbroker. He was a pretty cool guy with a huge house and a pool, and he sure seemed to be home an awful lot to enjoy it. I guess that was mostly during his FBI investigation, but still, his job seemed perfect.

Until offers poured in from various brokerage houses, I thought it wise to get a temporary job. You don't want to jump at the first thing, you know.

I filled out my application at Sunnyside Temps, and since I had basic computer skills, I landed a job in the office of the controller at Rockwell International. It was a big company that made parts for NASA and other stuff for the government. Best of all, Mrs. Manchester was happier than I'd seen her in weeks. She even loaned me money to get me started in my own $425-a-month beach studio on Balboa Boulevard. She said I didn't need to pay her back, but I was going to.

My job was to sit there, occasionally answer the phone, sit there, say my boss wasn't available, and sit there. There weren't even any windows to daydream out of, only a six-month-old issue of *Cosmopolitan*. The last secretary had already filled out all the sex quizzes. Judging by her answers, Dexter should give this woman a call.

On the last page, I paused at a Negro college foundation ad: *a mind is a terrible thing to waste.* Amen, brother.

I decided to keep my mind active and write a few letters to friends to boast about my new job. I made twelve dollars an hour! That's right, way more than Barb, and I didn't even have to lift a finger. I saved my letters under three-character names like "bet," "net," and "get" so I could easily find, print, and delete them afterward.

With my envelopes licked and stamps stolen, it was time to purge the files. My boss would be back soon from his three-hour lunch. Return, return, return, CTRL F, B-E-T, ESC, return, CTRL F, N-E-T, return. The phone rang.

"I'm sorry, Mr. Halverson is still at lunch," I said, pushing Escape, Escape, Escape too many times in annoyance. By the time I hung up, the screen had turned from pretty blue to a blackish-green, save for a lone blinking cursor. Shit. Where was I? I tried CTRL F G-E-T. Nothing happened. Fuck. It wasn't letting me delete my letters any more. He'd be back any minute. Don't panic, deep breath. I had learned a foolproof command, D-E-L, that could instantly clear any problem you were having. I clacked D-E-L G-E-T.

A flashing alert threatened me. "If you do this, all access will be lost." I punched ENTER and folded my arms. Who reads those commands anyway? No computer was going to be in charge of me. The computer revved up. Never-before-seen icons streamed in continual rows across the screen.

"Stop! Wait! I'm sorry, Mr. Computer; I take it back." But it was too late.

The phone rang. "What happened on your terminal?" a man's voice screamed.

I reached behind the desk and unplugged the monitor. How the fuck did they know already?

"What's a terminal?" I covered the mouthpiece and exhaled, *Fuuuuuuuck.*

Telling the truth had never worked in the past. I would deny everything. I plugged the computer back in and helplessly watched the letters continue to race across the screen.

"What happened!" Mr. Halverson rushed in, his beeper pinging wildly.

"I dunno. I didn't do it."

"The entire mainframe is down."

Mr. Halverson jumped ass-first into his chair and massaged his keyboard, gurgling sounds deep from within. Sometimes he pulled out eyebrow hairs and yelled, "Fuck, fuck, fuck!" slapping the keyboard like a one-year-old playing the piano.

I stacked and unstacked papers and stared at the wall without saying a word while he had his tantrums. It was four thirty now. Dexter was at happy hour with forty bucks his mom gave us so she wouldn't have to cook us dinner. Dexter could give a shit about waiting for me. I needed to leave now.

"Sir, do you mind if I leave a little early today?" He shooed me away without looking up.

# Chapter 9

# Temp Is Short for Temporary

Come Monday morning, I hoped the good people at Rockwell would forget what my overly exuberant fingers had done.

"Jack, come in here." This couldn't be good. I put Mrs. Manchester's leftovers away in my desk drawer and tiptoed into his office.

"Yes, sir, did you need something?"

He kept his head down.

"His lame-ass secretary hasn't got shit to do. I wonder if he's fucking her," he read aloud.

Shit. He was reading my letters. I looked back for my coveted lunch of leftovers.

"Does this mean I'm fired?" I encouraged an octave higher, picturing Dexter and myself picnicking on the beach, staring at the ocean, wondering where life might take us next.

"Not a chance, Buster. You are staying here and inputting all the shit you deleted."

I guess, (well, actually, he told me by yelling,) that by repeatedly pushing "Escape," I had landed in DOS. D-E-L-G-E-T erased the first three letters of their access code "GET," which made their files float around freely on the hard drive with no way to pull them up.

I felt bad, really I did. I slaved away at his data entry for the next four days, waiting for the perfect time to point out that he should be thanking me that something like this would never happen again at Rockwell. But that time never came.

When Friday rolled around, he said, "I've called your service. Don't bother coming back on Monday."

Fuck! Oh well. On to the next temp service, with a valuable lesson learned: you need not put every job down on your resume.

I did feel fortunate, however, that the temp services don't send around faxes to each other, like Most Wanted posters. On Tuesday, I scored another job from an agency called Manpower, at a property management company.

I had a specific task this time. I was proofreading the maid's handbook for the Desert Inn in Las Vegas just before it went to print. This would keep me from leafing through bad magazines, and writing letters. Idle hands really are the devil's tools, and if Rockwell had kept me busy like this gig, nothing like that would have ever happened.

My work area was in the basement of a cement building, with only one window. I had a view of a bush this time. It was something, at least. I tried to feel shameful and remember Rockwell when I started in on the proofreading, but twenty minutes into it, I was bored out of my fucking mind. This new job was not only beneath me, but I was spell-checking a handbook for maids who should be living it up! Why follow stupid rules for minimum wage? There had to be one job on the planet where you could fuck around more than usual, sit on the bed, watch your soaps, and still have life be okay. So I decided to rewrite the handbook.

Page 27, Rules of Conduct: #10. If you walk in on a guest who is naked or in his underwear, dart your eyes toward his crotch. This is an excellent way to make extra cash in your new job.

#11. If there is cash lying around on the dresser, and you are not sure if it's your tip or not, it's not, so just take half and rearrange the rest.

#12. Make copies of your master key and share it with your favorite employees throughout the hotel. Make sure you get the freebies you deserve.

#13. Only clean the absolute minimum. This will give you extra time to catch up on your favorite TV shows.

#14. Only change the bedspread if there are noticeable body fluids on it. See #13. Let the other maids do your work.

#15. Finish high school, and get a better job. Your parents were right.

I continued on with a few more suggestions, attempting to inspire the one goody-goody who had read this far.

Just as I backed up the document on a floppy and sealed the manila envelope addressed to the printer, a deafening crack jolted me. Was God watching me? The walls jiggled like Jell-O and the filing cabinets jerked open and closed like props in an *Exorcist* sequel. Then someone yelled, "Earthquake!" That triggered a woman in the next room to shriek just as a potted plant leapt off the shelf and hit me square in the temple. I fell to my knees. I was going to be *super* pissed if I was going to die working in this shitty place at twenty-two. I now understood why they always shook and slapped the screaming lady in those old movies. It sure was annoying and just made everyone else more unsettled. But there was no time to find the Screaming Mimi. I was too scared. I ran outside to save my own skin, went straight to my Jeep and just started driving.

That night in my new studio, with an ice bag on my head, I watched Channel 2's complete coverage of the 6.2 magnitude Whittier quake on a plaid sleeper couch Dexter and I found abandoned behind Safeway. I imagined tomorrow's newspaper. I, of course, would make page 17. "Loser Male Secretary Put Out of Misery by Falling Fern." Secretary could now be officially crossed off my career list, along with mall whore, trucker, and male model. I needed to take some of my advice from the maid's handbook.

# Chapter 10

# "Real" Job Hunting

There were no temp agencies to find me a job as a stockbroker. So for the entire next day, I opened the yellow pages and called all the well-known brokerage firms, but I never even got past their receptionists. In the want ads, the only job remotely related to stockbroker was for a cold-caller at a local firm, Sutro and Company. I was desperate for money and frustrated, so I drove up to Sutro at Fashion Island Shopping Center and walked straight into their office. The first person I saw was a man whose belt curved below the bubble of his massive stomach like a smiley face.

"I'm here for the cold-calling job," I said.

"You think you have what it takes, son?"

"Yes, sir."

"Let me introduce you to Chip," the man said, walking me along the wine-colored carpet through the sparsely populated cubicles of the main room to a rear corner office.

Chip had sandy hair and a freckled face. He looked like a kid that would kiss your mom's ass to her face, and then clean out the cookie jar when she wasn't looking, leaving you to take all the blame.

I reached out to shake his hand, but instead he folded his arms and stared at me.

"I can't exactly pay you, Jack, but I'll give you 10 percent of the gross if anything pans out."

"How much is that?" I asked.

"Two thousand a month, no problem. Once you get the hang of it."

That was a fortune, especially all lumped into one sum like that. The red rash under his left nostril from years of picking boogers worried me that he might be full of shit. But I had no other job and nothing to lose. At least it was a real office, with a phone and everything. I needed this chance. I imagined Mrs. P's face sneering down at me, so I sat, fists clenched, ready to be the best smile-and-dialer Chip had ever seen.

"Why don't you start with this?" Chip grinned. He plopped down the phone directory for a nearby retirement community called "Leisure World." The first "L" had been angrily scratched over into an "S."

I tried to remain upbeat during my dials to Leisure World, especially when I could actually speak to someone without yelling, but that's when the prospect usually told me I was the fourth or fifth broker to have called that day. I was getting sad.

However, it was interesting to experience everyone's unique style of getting off the phone. One little old lady I called said, "What's that? khhrrrrrrrrrr, we must have a bad connection." Then she hung up on me. I would have wanted to party with her fifty years ago, for sure.

But why was Chip setting me up like this? He must have known old people weren't sitting ducks. They had seen it all. Maybe this was a test? I grabbed the Irvine phone book instead and searched for nice sounding streets, finding gems like Copper Cloud Way and Tranquility Drive. No contractor would have the balls to build a crappy tract house on a street with names like that.

Lo and behold, by the end of the day, I had three qualified leads that agreed to speak with Chip. My plan was working until the next call gristled, "Who the hell do you think you are, interrupting my dinner?" I heard a strange click and a husky-voiced woman started moaning,

"Ooooh, yeah. You know you want it."

"I do not want it, and you can't make me!" the cold-call lead from Majestic Palm Terrace screeched back. I looked over to Chip's muffled laughter behind his glass wall and hung up.

"What the hell was that? I almost had her."

"Listen, rookie. When the cold calls get nasty like that, you gotta give 'em the 976 treatment. Keep your self-respect." The 976 phone calls were those pay-by-the-minute phone calls. I looked to the ground. Right now I sure wished Spokane was enough for me.

"You've got to be in control. Deal with these folks in a military fashion. Like this." Chip pushed play on a handheld tape recorder.

"But—" I said.

"But nothing. Listen."

There was mumbling and squeaking furniture.

"What is this?" I huffed. I was in no mood for a motivational speech from some smarty-pants. The recording played, sounding like wood pounding on wood. More moans and grunts.

"What is this?"

"It's me and my ex. Shhh. This is the part where I bang her head against the headboard."

I leaned up against the glass wall encasing his office and kept time with the recording by tapping my head against the solid glass, thinking this might help me understand his lesson. A framed picture of Chip and a tanned girl wearing a woven sombrero caught my eye. I reached for it on his desk.

"Is that her? She's pretty." I reverted to my ass-kissing days with Mrs. Pohlkiss, where a simple compliment about her dress or hair could usually snap her out of a tirade.

"No. Sit down. You're gonna love this story even more." Chip turned off the tape and started talking nonstop about sombrero girl and their date down to Ensenada, Mexico.

"So anyway, we're on our way back, and I decided to eat in Puerto Nuevo for the five-buck lobsters. There was no way that girl was getting a full-priced one from me back home. Looking at ceramic piggy banks all day works up an appetite, ya know. So anyway, all day long I had to listen to her talk about nothing. The only time she stopped was when she was stuffing a big chunk of the buttery rubber lobster in her mug. And that's when I see the fire extinguisher on the wall."

"Was there a fire?" I asked.

"Don't interrupt me. So I said, 'You ever had a frosty?' And she said, 'No what's that?'"

"So that's when I blasted her with it." Phil held an imaginary fire hose and sprayed it at me with sound effects. "Turned everything but her greasy chin as white as Frosty the Snowman."

Chip cackled and slapped me hard on the back, trying to beat a laugh out of me, but I stayed silent. I would be the subject of his next story.

"Boy, was she pissed on the way home," he snorted.

"I can imagine."

"I did manage to talk her into giving me a Hoover just after Tijuana, though."

"Oh."

"Treat 'em mean, keep 'em keen, I always say."

I kept nodding.

"So you get what I'm saying now?" He stung my back with another slap.

"Words to live by. If you want to be an asshole."

"What did you say, Jack?"

"Nothing."

"Hey, you know how to find the hole on a fat girl?"

I shook my head.

"You roll her in flour. That's where I got the idea for the extinguisher, dummy." Chip went to slap me again, but I grabbed his hand and crunched his fingers until he winced. I crunched them hard for me, and for the lobster girl.

"I'm not paying to entertain you. Get back on the phone," he said, shaking out his fingers.

I hobbled back to the safety of my cubicle and put my face in my hands, painfully realizing that I really didn't have anything better to offer the competition, except my boss would give you a "frosty" if you talked too much.

Even outside of work there was nothing to look forward to. Dexter got in a mac daddy fight with his mom, and she cut off his happy hour allowance that we both counted on. Tonight I would have to eat happy hour food alone at the Red Onion and hope they'd let me slide because I couldn't even afford a drink.

## Chapter 11

# October 19, 1987

I should have never gone back for another week with Chip. It was the day the stock market fell 23 percent, more than the drop in 1929 before the Great Depression. Chip twirled his venetian blinds shut and hid in his office while I fielded countless calls from his enraged clients wondering why Chip hadn't sold everything in their portfolio at the high. This sucked.

Regular TV was canceled for nonstop coverage of the financial ruin. A few people even jumped off buildings, which got me thinking, if you were going to kill someone and get away with it, today would be the day to toss them out the window.

Even Drexel Burnham Lambert, one of the most respected firms that rose to greatness in the last few years—one where I couldn't even get past the receptionist—went tits up overnight. Who would listen to someone from a no-name firm like us if Drexel went out of business?

"Time to dial for dollars," Chip said, plopping down a stack of account statements.

"Where'd you get these?"

"Dumpster diving behind Merrill last night. They even have phone numbers."

"Where are you going?" I asked.

"That's none of your business," he said, putting a white Adidas warm-up jacket over his collared shirt.

I had to do it. My rent was due. But I needed lunch first. There were no more Mrs Manchester's leftovers to cheer me up. I threw together a homemade Budig meat sandwich. You know, the really cheap pressed meat that tastes like cold salt.

I searched the clutter of my desk for a magazine to use as a placemat. This would make my shitty lunch seem more civilized. I went about busily squirting yellow mustard packs on the bread, because I *love* yellow mustard. It was something that reminded me of home. Not just the mustard, but the squeeze packs it came in. Mom always saved an assortment of packets in the fridge from whenever we got fast food.

A big glop of mustard jizzed on my *Newsweek*. It was then I noticed the cover, "The Best Paying Jobs of 1987." I'd sure like one of those, I thought, flipping to the center. Among them: brain surgeon and selling arms to the Contras, but another one was selling bonds. That was it! I could still fulfill my dream of having a big fat house with a pool, but unlike these silly stocks, bonds would always provide some kind of return until they matured. Chip said to never ever use the word "always" in our business, but what did he know?

I had one small problem. I didn't have any money to move to New York or anywhere else to trade bonds, for that matter. So it was back to the Yellow Pages. There was only one listing for a bond firm in town, Freedom Capital Markets. With a name like that, they had to have integrity, right?

Every day for a week, I called Freedom and flirted with the receptionist. On Friday, I was actually granted an interview! I was serious this time. Deep inside my duffle was my only suit, with a red rubber band around it. Mom bought it for Gramps just before he died. He hated it and made her promise she wouldn't bury him in it. I put it on and headed toward my destiny.

The blue wool three-piece suit was a little tight and itchy, but the interview went like magic. The chubby fifty-year-old pockmarked man seemed very pleased that I had a college education.

"Gonzag-ee. Is that like a Kinman Business University?"

"Um, I guess so."

"My niece took a class there once."

"Does she still go there?"

"No, she's pregnant now."

"Oh."

"You don't have any babies floating around out there, do you?"

"No, sir."

"Good man. Do you know anything about the bond market?"

"Well, not really." My eyes sank with my heart.

"Not a problem. We've got a real fine training program here. You'll be taught by the best."

"Does that mean I'm hired?"

"I don't see why not."

Ka-ching! Gonzaga finally paid off for real! I got my first bona fide job! As soon as his office door closed behind me, I jumped up, punched my fist in the air and screamed a silent "*Yes!*"

I was floating on my way out. I stopped to gaze onto the austere one-hundred-person trading floor and smiled at the backs of all my new friends, sitting with their phones glued to their heads. I couldn't wait to start my two weeks of training. I was determined to become one of them.

# Chapter 12

# Training Camp

"Jack and Alice, you two, come with me," said a bitchy young secretary in the reception area at Freedom Capital on Monday morning. She was not the one I flirted with on the phone. She ushered me and my fellow trainee into a conference room with a massive glossy table. A television and a VCR resting on an elevated metal stand hugged the far corner.

"Take notes if you want," she said, placing two legal pads in front of us before teetering out of the room on her stilettos.

Alice and I shrugged and decided to get to know each other while we waited for our instructor.

"This is my ticket to the beachfront," Alice said, standing at the floor to ceiling windows. Her athletic legs and perfect breasts made her look amazing in her red skirt.

"Can you believe how lucky we are?" I stared out into the white-yellow sky toward where mountains on a clear day were promised. "I mean, Freedom is really investing in us."

"Baby, they've got nothing to lose hiring us," Alice said, shaking her head.

"What do you mean?" I said. I looked to the closed door. They better not catch her talking like that.

The door opened.

"Umm. Like, it's been a half hour. Don't you think you guys should start?" The receptionist bitched like a Valley Girl.

"Where's the instructor?" I asked.

The receptionist let out a loud annoyed sigh and marched over to the metal stand and turned on the electronics.

"Right here." She pointed to the television before speeding out of the room, huffing like she was *very* busy and important. I knew better.

Our "real fine training program" was a homemade video emceed by fifty-five-year-old Jim Graham, who, as of last Friday, had left the firm to start a Merry-Maid franchise.

Through the episodes, Jim wore a rainbow of Polo shirts. His brown Sally Jesse Raphael glasses magnified his eyes like Mr. Magoo, which made it hard to take him seriously as he read aloud from various financial education manuals to his on-screen class of six.

It was clear that he too was learning this stuff for the first time. If a student dared to ask a question, which would almost always make him lose his place in his book, he would scream at them full force until his face turned red.

"No questions! You are here to learn! Stop talking!" Then he'd blink for a pregnant minute until he calmed himself down enough to clear his throat before he began to read again. His face got even redder if someone dared to ask another question during his recovery minute. That would make him pound his fists on the table and growl at them, resetting his internal blink clock back at zero, seemingly to annoy them, like driving behind a slow driver on a skinny road. It sure annoyed Alice and me.

"That Troy guy is about to ask another one." Alice stayed glued to the screen. It was like the longest *Saturday Night Live* skit, ever.

On the seventh day, the skit was finally over. Jim threw his hands up and picked up his gold watch, which he rested on the table in front him.

"Well. This is my fifth time through this stuff. I still don't get it. And I'm pretty damn smart. They're nuts if they think you dummies can learn it all in two weeks." He glanced at his watch again. "I'm late for my tee time. You're just going to have to pick it up out there in the trenches."

And with that, he rose and tripped on the table leg, nearly toppling the camera.

"Goddammit!" he yelled, looking back, like someone had moved the camera in his way. Then the screen went blue. I hadn't learned a thing. I was just glad it was over.

# Chapter 13

# The Trenches

My employment papers gave me a loan for $1,200 a month, for the first three months. Alice got $4,000 because of her experience. I really wasn't that jealous. She just had to pay back more money after they took their 60 percent cut. It wasn't as easy as it sounded, but a few people made it look that way.

Everyone knew who was a "producer" and who was on borrowed time. A white magic marker board behind the trading desk boasted the current month's Top 10. Thor, who changed his name from Cletus when he moved out from Arkansas, was the winner so far this month at $150,000, followed closely by Patrick Sweeney and Ben Wyndham. That left the rest of us borrowed-timers to scowl at them like jealous child beauty pageant mothers desperate to figure out their winning secrets.

I spun around slowly in my chair. My cubicle was smack dab in the center of the trading floor. I stared at the ceiling, numbed by the sea of chattering voices, each ignoring each other, like a grand convention of schizophrenics in training. Every furnishing in the room was gray, including the phones, all lit by florescent lights, which added to my wooziness. I realized I would have to cold call and be rejected by thousands of people, even if this time the clients were mine to keep.

In the cubicle to my left hovered Ron Mac Ilroy from Texas. Nearly bald at twenty-six, he wasn't quite ready to let go of the parted-down-the-middle spiked gel look that made his scalp look like a drought-stricken wheat crop.

"Gonzaga? Sounds like the kind of VD I got back in Abilene." Ron laughed and slapped his knee before wiping an imaginary tear. "Never heard of that school. I got my associate's in home economics at Texas Christian," he said, outstretching his arms and cracking his knuckles over his head. "Momma was right. Smartest fucking major. I got so much pussy that year."

Only in Texas could you major in learning how to be a better wife for your man.

Much of the day, Ron burned up our free Watts line to his friends back home, not fully understanding that this job was 100 percent commission. I didn't care if he wasn't working, but it was really hard to concentrate on cold calling when instead I could listen to Ron apologizing to his live-in girlfriend for smacking her around the night before, or to him flirting with a new girl he'd just met in the checkout line at Lucky's.

"Your melons were making my carrot so hard when I saw you in the produce section," he told her. Really, no lie, he said that.

It was much better than anything on TV. It made me realize that unlike the obvious freaks trying to keep me down (like Mrs. Pohlkiss), Ron was a new and dangerous species. His kind were plentiful here at Freedom, types who specialized in pushing me off course from my fortune, just by existing.

There was also Danny, who sat in front of me. He was Ron's meticulously dressed training room buddy. Danny had just leased a shiny black VW Golf with his first draw check, complete with the personalized license plate, "GQGOLFER," telling the world, in case they couldn't immediately guess, that he looked like a model and played a damn fine round of golf. I never really understood personalized plates. Nobody in Spokane had them. But here it seemed like people had them if you wanted to be pulled over and fucked on the side of the road: NSTYGRL, IPUTOUT, FATSLUT, or BIGPNIS.

Danny's Golf was optioned with a motion-sensitive alarm, complete with a keychain beeper that alerted him in case anyone tried to meddle with his ride. This started an officewide game of sending someone down to the parking lot to jiggle the car. Then we'd watch Danny dash downstairs in his crispy suit to catch the thief. In some way, it was comforting to know I wasn't the only one easily distracted from the pain of calling random angry strangers, but this game was getting ridiculous.

Soon the entire office was taking over/under bets on how many minutes Danny's round trip would take him. This lasted about a week until an "over" bettor got clever and stalled all the elevators in the lobby. Danny had to run down and up eleven flights of stairs. When Danny returned, huffing and puffing in his pitted-out suit to cries of foul play by outraged "under" bettors, he finally wised up and disabled his alarm.

It was back to Ron for my distraction fix.

"I'm calling women only from here on out!" Ron said, probably longing for his days back in home ec. "They think I'm irresistible. And I'm in control." Ron clenched his jaw and jammed his thumb to his chest to convince himself. Maybe he just thought he could smack the women around for a few trades once they were under his spell.

But I'll admit, Ron's knack for telling these unknown women he'd never met in person, "you sure are purty," was genius—because it worked. The next week Ron wrote his first ticket, a three-year CD with $750 commission, thanks to a nice sixty-year-old lady who ran a small credit union in Sugar Land, Texas.

"Tell people what they want to hear, and you'll go far," Ron gloated, filling out his first trade ticket. He snapped the ticket in my face like a crisp dollar bill. I was *super* jealous and outraged. This goofball was leaving me in the dust. I was almost ready to commit myself to his plan until he cheapened it by calling his mother.

"Momma?! Guess what?!"

Ron's face turned angry.

"Dammit, Momma! We ain't pregnant! We hyperspaced that thing a month ago. I told you that. I'm fixing to get mad; let's try this again. Momma! Guess what?" He paused. "That's better. I am a bond broker!"

I could tell by Ron's smile that Momma hadn't been this proud since he'd passed his devil's food cake exam. The asshole had finally popped his cherry.

After your first trade at Freedom, tradition allowed one of the important people to cut your tie in half and tape it on the trading board. Then you were in the club. Kind of like in *National Geographic*, where in Africa if you married a virgin, you got to hang the bloody sheet in front of your hut to prove it.

Ron was so pumped up after Momma's call, he couldn't wait. He grabbed the scissors from his pen holder and darted up to the elevated trading desk, handing them to the first trader he saw.

"Wyatt, can you do the honors?" Ron asked.

Fat Wyatt quickly cut Ron's tie, shooed him away with the back of his hand, and went back to reading his magazine. After only the knot remained, Ron pranced around the room with the remnant held high, shaking the hand of anyone who gave him eye contact. He saved the producers for last. They sat in a special aisle away from us commoners with a view of the 405 Freeway.

"I'm gonna get me one of them black SLs, like you Thor."

Thor, the blond-haired leader of the producers, looked back at his court like a five-year-old who had just been kissed by his sharp whiskered aunt.

"Hold up. This isn't a bond trade," Thor said.

"Whadya mean?" Ron asked.

"This is a CD trade. Any dumb shit can do one of those. Now you just sit back down there and get on the phone." Thor pointed to Ron's chair.

The rest of the producers nodded. Thor stood up. He wasn't finished with Ron yet.

"Where's your tie, boy? We have a dress code here."

Ron held up what was left of his tie to Thor.

"Should we send him home to get it?" Thor asked, provoking more chuckles from his club.

In this live version of *Go to the Head of the Class*, Ron wasn't allowed to move his board piece to the top row just yet. Ron sat back down and put the ruined tie away in his drawer without even looking over at me.

He picked up his phone. But instead of calling Momma back, he called his girlfriend and started a fight with her to make himself feel better, yelling something about the place being a mess and what a shitty cook she was, and how everything that happened today was all her fault.

Ron never did get a chance to do a real trade. He was fired two weeks later for nonproduction. More likely, the producers didn't want *him* to be one of them.

It was hard for me to lead such a low-profile life, keeping my social Tourette's in check and all, but after Ron, it became clear that if you spread your wings too far, you'd get shot down, just for the fun of it. The producers might employ slower, more painful ways of weeding you out after your three months draw expired. Like starving you.

Danny knew his head was next on the chopping block. He was of little use to the Thor Squad after he quit reacting to his car alarm. But he wasn't going down without a fight. Instead of leaving when they stopped his draw, he decided to get a night job at JC Penney and continue at Freedom by day.

"Jack, are you aware that JC Penney sells more drapery than any other retailer?" Danny asked me. He was trying to find the good in what he was doing. I knew my brother's pain, watching the hundreds of thousands of dollars the other boobs were making. He thought his big break was just around the corner, but the corner just kept getting farther and farther away.

As the weeks wore on, Danny's suits were no longer freshly pressed. The rings under his eyes darkened. He was giving up hope. He was the first of many guys I watched completely lose their self-confidence, wondering why this elusive success never happened for them. They were left to walk out the door, dejected, alone, and really fucking exhausted. There were no going-away parties. I was determined never to leave Freedom this way. I would not—could not—fail.

# Chapter 14

# Man's Business

Alice had already opened up three new accounts that were generating more than enough to cover her draw. She knew I was trying my heart out, so after every one of the trades she so effortlessly executed, she'd come over and give me a quick back rub. It was her way of sharing the feeling, putting some good karma in my bank before the rest of the office tried to beat it out of her. After her inaugural trade, since she wasn't wearing a tie, one of the traders offered to cut the cotton panel out of her panty hose and tape it on the trading board.

"Sorry, Jim, I'm wearing my knee-highs today," she said, lifting up her blue business slacks just high enough to prove it with a snap of the elastic cuff before slowly lowering her pant hem with a pleasant, blank-faced stare that could have killed an army.

This was definitely a man's business. Any woman would have to take these comments, and more, in stride if she wanted to make the big bucks. In this world it took a certain savvy and finesse to be a successful woman and not be labeled a "chick with a dick." Alice was gaining that respect at lightning speed. She was my hero.

There were only two other surviving women brokers, Tiffany Wong and Debra Riley. The first week I was on the floor, everyone was talking shit about Tiffany being fresh back from a little elective surgery funded by a recent home-run trade. She was only twenty-nine. She didn't want to miss too much work, so she chose a package deal done all at once: eyes rounded, breasts enlarged, and a bridge put in her nose to go with her freshly dyed sandy blonde hair, all so that she wouldn't look Asian any more. It must have sucked growing up in Orange County, feeling ostracized by so many perfect white airheads. Now she could afford to be—almost—one of them.

That left thirty-year-old Debra, who probably *should* have had some kind of surgery. She sported greasy blonde braided pigtails that made her the spitting image of the little evil girl from *The Bad Seed*.

"I only have to wash my hair every two weeks," she bragged to Alice near the water cooler. Then she gave her scalp a good scratch and set free molting chunks of dandruff that she flicked off her fingernails like lint. Maybe it was because none of the sexual comments in the office were directed at her, but each time Debra overheard one, I could see her wince. After the cotton panel incident, she tried to get close with Alice.

"You know, Alice, you should keep a journal. Like me." Debra showed Alice her blue Mead spiral notebook. "Bad Things" was scrawled on the front. "Just in case you have a couple slow months and those guys need a little coaxing to keep your draw."

Debra handed it to Alice.

"I didn't have to work for a year after my last job at the county, if you know what I mean," Debra boasted.

Silly Debra. Alice didn't need to blackmail anyone. She would be sitting on producers' row before Debra's next hair washing, and not have to talk to her any longer.

It was a huge bummer when Debra started being nice to me. She saw what good pals Alice and I were and must have thought I'd be her good luck charm too. I liked it better when she just ignored me, so I pretended not to notice her hanging out at the Sparkletts water cooler, where we avoided the milky white So Cal water. It was the only free thing that Freedom gave us. But doggonit, on this particular trip to the water cooler, it was impossible to avoid watching Debra gingerly handle Tiffany's new breasts.

"They'll soften up in a few weeks; don't worry," Debra said with a nurse's authority, moving her healing fingers to Tiffany's bandaged nose.

"I wish they didn't stop using silicon," Tiffany lamented. Leaky Dow Corning boob implants were sickening women; it was all over the news. A new law required doctors to only use implants filled with saltwater, but they just didn't squish the same.

"Jack! Oh, good." Debra caught me while I was still transfixed by Tiffany's new breasts.

"I want to let you in on something really exciting," Debra said in a creepy flirty way, pulling me by my shirt collar until I was an inch from her crazed gaze. Why did Debra's breath smell like a fried fish filet sandwich?

All of a sudden I was thrust back into third grade at St. Al's. It was just after lunch on fish Friday, and I had just finished my mac 'n' cheese. Big fat Shelly Franken was forcing me back into the cloak room, lifting up her plaid uniform skirt to show me her Bo Bo without warning.

"Look at it!" she insisted. After that, she tried to take all the Red Hots that Mom had packed in my Road Runner lunch box as payment. I negotiated her down to just three cinnamon pebbles, but even at that price, I felt like I'd been tricked into buying something I really didn't want.

With that scar reopened, I didn't know what Debra had up her sleeve. I thought maybe she might guide *my* hand to touch Tiffany's new boobs and then call out to the manager until I gave her an account on my protected list. This was why I got even more tense when Debra started telling me about EST—some mind control seminar where Debra must have ended up walking on coals after she told a thousand people how her Uncle Bob stuck it to her when she was ten, and then broke down in convulsive tears with her nostrils flaring and snot running down her face as the emcee loudspeakered, "*Next!*"

I must have been Debra's first sales pitch victim after the seminar. After they'd put some kind of spell or incredible guilt trip on her to bring in other plebes to pay the huge seminar fee for the chance of getting over a lifetime of shit in one weekend. Apparently the empowered feeling would wear off if she didn't find a sucker to get her in for free the next time. It sounded a lot like selling Amway, except you got to cry.

"Oh, Jack, you would be *so good* at it." She touched my arm, making my hair stand on end. "The way you feel at the end, just telling the world the whole truth about your life." I didn't have an Uncle Bob.

"Debra, I think it's a scam."

Her left eye fluttered.

"You're an assface!" she screamed. Her fists clenched at her sides, furious I was denying her free accolades from her Holiday Inn Jim Jones. She walked to her cubicle, sat down, and opened her journal. She darted her eyes at me, then scribbled frantically. Fuck her for thinking I was an easy mark.

I guess I could just add her to the growing list of friends I hadn't made at work. To them, I was just another annoying short-timer like Danny or Ron, only worse because I couldn't afford a car alarm or bake a cake.

Even life outside of work had fallen in the shitter. Dexter couldn't fake the goody-goody part of his double life anymore. After a final showdown with his mom, he moved to San Francisco to make his own fortune. He was so pissed that he didn't even call me to let me know until he got there. It was beyond disaster for me. I had no one left in town. He disappeared overnight.

I was lonely and broke with a forty-year-old woman for a best friend, and she wouldn't even go out to the bars with me.

"Come on, just one drink," I pleaded to Alice.

"People would think I hired you," she said as she caressed my chin.

Dating fresh young girls was out of the question too. I didn't have a dollar to my name, and Mrs. Manchester's house was gone to me. Most importantly, I didn't have a wingman to legitimize my game. In my own sad little way, I had become just like my cousin Barb now—unfuckable.

However, I did get a little desperate one afternoon and followed through on Alice's advice of scrounging the happy hour at the Red Onion. I ended up with a thirty-eight-year-old tourist who was happy to buy me drinks so she could relive her youth—something I would still recommend for any starving twenty-two-year-old. But for me, nothing could bounce me out of my sadness. I still had that nagging human condition of wanting to be accepted and liked by everyone—even if they all sucked.

# Chapter 15

# Shiny, Happy People

The next day I went to work determined to score, and was able to stay on the phone the entire day without distraction. When it was over, I hopped into the elevator and smiled at the meanest trader—fat Wyatt. Everyone knew he was trying to dry out this week. Boy, were his nerves on edge! I waited patiently inside the elevator while he held the door open and lectured another broker on the sure-fire direction of interest rates. The elevator door closed. It seemed to be the perfect time to cheer him up with a little of my new inner light. The red Emergency Stop button winked at me. Pulling it would be a clever way to make him laugh—we would all become instant friends. His angry scowls would end. I pulled the button.

"Woop! Woop!"

The alarm sounded and our car jerked to a bungy cord-like stop. Sweat beaded on Wyatt's fat purple forehead. His bulbous alcoholic nose got even redder.

"It's people like you that make me need a drink!" He steadied himself on the railing of the bobbing car.

*Like I'm the reason you're a big, fat boozer*, I thought, trying to reinsert the broken button.

"Give me that damn thing." Wyatt went for the button in my hand.

"I can do it." I instinctively put it behind my back. I pushed him away with my free arm and bent my knees up and down to make the car sway to scare him away.

"You're gonna make the elevator fall, jumping like that." Wyatt froze, barely breathing. But then he lunged for me, grabbing the button. In the scuffle, it fell to the ground.

"You're trying to kill us," Wyatt sweated.

I placed my foot on top of the button, hoping to buy myself an extra moment to win it back, but a crunching sound made it clear it was gone for good.

"You guys okay in there?" a voice from a speaker said.

"We just stepped out for coffee," I said.

"Get me out of here!" Wyatt screamed. "Oh no. Oh no!" Wyatt put a hand on his butt and walked around in a circle. And then the most disgusting, unthinkable thing happened. Wyatt took off his wingtip shoe, pulled down his pants, squatted and took a shit in his shoe. I immediately took off my dress shirt and tied it around my face like a bandit mask.

"What are you looking at? I'm nervous." Wyatt said.

The stink made for a very long hour and a half while being locked up in that metal box with my new buddy waiting for the fire department to rescue us. The good news was that, with Wyatt shitting in his shoe, we agreed to not mention anything to anyone. The instant the door opened, Wyatt took off running with his poo-filled shoe tucked under his arm, and that was it.

# Chapter 16

# Morning Y'All

And so it went. Day after day, I crept into the mandatory morning meetings at five forty-five to listen to the head trader, Rick from Arkansas, bark out a few highlights from the *Wall Street Journal*, something that any of us could calmly read ourselves. It was much more painful than sitting through church daydreaming. At least in church, the priest would end with, "Go in peace," to snap me out of my trance. Rick, on the other hand, would raise his hand over his head and yell, "Buy bonds; wear diamonds!" before dropping his hand down like a race car flag to flatten his greasy comb-over.

Now mind you, I wasn't above a good ass-kissing to better my position in the firm. And after the elevator incident, I assumed Wyatt was probably bad-mouthing me to Rick. So I took it upon myself to sound fascinated with anything Rick would say, even if it meant listening to the same stories over and over.

"Back home in Little Rock, in the good old days"—which meant three years ago to Jim—"if you had a 100k month, you got to go down to Parker Porsche and pick out any ride you wanted."

"Wow, Rick, really? Any ride?" It was kind of interesting the first time, but not the sixth.

"That's right. Any ride. Only one per year, though," he'd cock his head to side and say with a "darn" face, maintaining it until I cocked my head to the side and matched his expression. I was convinced that being a bond broker in the South was the equivalent to being a movie star. Maybe snuggling with Alain might not have been so bad after all? At least I could have slept in

But to my surprise, through some of Rick's stories I began to understand more about the economy than I ever expected to know. Like how yields up meant prices down, and other things I just memorized to pass tests in Econ. But you didn't need a college education to understand why savings and loan banks were going broke every day. People were walking away from their homes and businesses because they were worth less than the loan.

Because of this, the Federal Home Loan Bank devised an S&L bailout program known as FICO, which stood for Financing Corporation of America. FICO had no assets but carried an implied guarantee from the government, which was good enough for an implied AAA rating by the two main rating services, Moody's and Standard & Poor. That was more than good enough for me. The would-be investors were supposed to take this rating on faith and just feel good about their part in cleaning up the massive financial mess.

In early summer of 1988, FICO issued several billion dollars in zero coupon STRIPS, which was short for separate trading of registered interest and principle of securities. In other words, bonds that don't pay interest until maturity. "Issued" meant investors give FICO money, and then FICO agreed to pay them back at a specified interest rate they dreamed up. It was a game of "who gets to house the crazy relative." No one wanted to touch them on issue day, and spreads widened to the yield of many junk bonds.

This was a rare opportunity for a place like Freedom to make money because no one knew exactly where the market was.

In these special few days, Freedom's traders could effortlessly make money by tying up an attractive offer to buy a block of FICO bonds on one line and then simultaneously sell them to a better buyer on the other line in a riskless transaction. It was free money, just for making a few phone calls, and it was legal. The only potential punishment was being cut off from the dealers if they ever found out you were middling them.

"Aren't you worried about being found out?" I asked Rick.

"Jack, think of it this way: these New York securities dealers are like a friend of yours asking you to watch their girlfriend when they are out of town for the weekend. So you decide to go ahead and fuck the girl yourself, because they're really not your friend anyway." Rick explained.

The salesmen at the large primary security dealers buying and selling these bonds to Freedom were making commission too, so who was going to tell?

# Chapter 17

# My Hero

Alice didn't need such antics to pull off her business. Her main client, the largest insurance company in Iowa, admired her spunk, and, contrary to the rest of the jealous office, she hadn't tasted theirs. I watched in awe as she gave her client a one-minute education on FICOs, then calmly hung up the phone, and yelled out an order for $30,000,000. That day she made $150,000, the price of a sweet four-bedroom house *with* a pool on the South Hill of Spokane. Her customer didn't even bother to put her in competition. My fellow trainee was definitely one of "them" now!

But only one week later, when I was sure she was a lifer, she suddenly quit.

"Baby, this job sucks, the hours suck, people at Freedom suck, and I want to keep my cotton panel."

"You're on the board, Alice! What are you thinking?"

"People are going to go to jail over this. I'd die in there without a man to take care of my business," she said. "Plus, my new boyfriend doesn't like these hours."

It was a gut punch—like watching Dad go off to war, leaving me to slug out life all on my own.

"What about me? I thought I was your new man."

"Don't worry. I'll be there for you if you really need me," she said, tousling my hair and kissing my forehead. There was no changing her mind.

"Do me a favor, Jack."

"Anything you want."

"Stay away from Wyatt."

Was love of her new boyfriend more important than this job? I sure hoped to fall in love and find out some day. That afternoon, Alice confidently strode off the trading floor with her head held high for the last time. The entire trading floor watched her go in silence.

# Chapter 18

# All in the Family

The owners of Freedom Capital, the Lincoln family, nattered near the office kitchen in shock and annoyance that someone would quit after being so successful. This had never happened before. They were in charge of the privilege of staying and the joy of firing.

The entire Lincoln clan was on the payroll at Freedom, including the wife, whose business card said, "Designer" as her job position. Mrs. Lincoln was the one responsible for decorating our office in the inspired gray theme. She had just donated a lithograph from her home of a woman with black hair, big arched eyebrows, and red lipstick.

"It's a Nagel," she snapped, looking away from the group at the mandatory-attendance ribbon-cutting ceremony, embarrassed at the big favor she was doing us.

After we gave her a round of insincere golf claps, she introduced our newest receptionist, their cousin Cammy, from Indiana. She could make her gum pop like firecrackers inside her mouth. It really rounded out our new nail salon atmosphere.

"You like that, huh?" Cammy smiled, as I stared, fixated on her red-lipped mouth wondering what other kind of objects had been worked around that orifice back home on the farm.

# Chapter 19

# Ho-Down

Every year, as a special treat for all us worker bees, the Lincoln family threw a Fourth of July party in their monstrous, florally decorated home. The house had large, white, round columns that didn't support anything but the small roof of the porch of the circular driveway. It was located in the grandest of all tracts, Nellie Gail Ranch, overlooking the twenty lane I-5 freeway in Mission Viejo.

All the guests arrived clean, with sugar smiles and outlandish compliments. That lasted until the drinks were overserved, and everyone was transformed back into trailer trash. I realized I too might be getting a bit sloshed, when I found myself entranced by a woman's back whose tight bra created two small sets of boobs near her armpits.

At no time in my life—even if I was best friends with the girl—was bra popping *ever* okay. But I was too buzzed to stop myself this time. Just a quick little snap to see how the small back boobs would react. She jerked around like an agitated dog chasing its tail. I ducked the opposite way, leaving her to shoot her look of disgust at that asshole Wyatt. Wyatt thought she was just flirting with him and responded by holding up his beer can to toast her.

"Hey, there, crazy." Her demeanor changed instantly. She cozied up to him, pleased that a man of power was the culprit. "You could have just said 'hello.'"

I was pressing my luck. I spied a random door that led me down some stairs to an underground wine cellar. Here sat the Lincolns' twenty-something balding son, doing bong hits, while he gazed through a bright baby blue glowing window that looked into the deep end of the pool.

"Hey." He nodded, and got back to staring for the next employee to jump in so he could watch their bathing suit fall down.

Wyatt cannonballed into the pool next and unknowingly blocked the window with his huge hairy back. He began to create a Jacuzzi of fart bubbles. I really couldn't blame him, though. The three Costco hot dogs I'd wolfed down weren't sitting so well with me either, insisting they wanted to go for a swim in a smaller, more private porcelain pool. I let out a stinky test fart to calm those ornery monsters down. The son didn't blink an eye.

I crept out of his cave and slunk my way up two floors of plush powder blue carpeting to find the master bathroom. That way there would be a room between me and the rest of the party to dissipate the guaranteed stench.

I creaked open one side of the hollow paneled white double door. There on the bed was the topless, recently promoted, ultra-important receptionist straddling Daddy Lincoln, who had his pants around his ankles. He was fondling her breasts with one hand and pleasuring his little smoky sausage with his other hand.

The door creak made Daddy panic. He grabbed for his glasses on the flowered orange bedspread.

"Honey, is that you? One of our guests got a splinter." The receptionist shrieked, covered her boobs and fell face-down on the bedspread. Daddy furiously pulled his pants over his white legs. I shut the door and scanned the open hallway, choosing instead to run downstairs and pretend nothing happened.

The most painful part, other than I was about to shit my pants, was that I had no one to share this juicy tidbit with. Surely I would be turned in by a loyal employee, eager to gain a tier on the Freedom caste system.

Downstairs, things were just as ugly. People's drunken voices sounded like snarling rabid dogs over the music, and the bathroom line was now three deep. I walked around, letting out more test farts to buy my bowels a few more minutes. It was fun to watch people accuse each other with their sour glances. But then even better entertainment came along.

Thor had bumped a blonde woman into the pool. Her thin white polyester dress was now see-through, and she wasn't wearing any underwear!

"Thor! You did that on purpose!" the woman's enraged husband, an almost producer, sputtered. He followed Thor into the kitchen and was ready to fight.

Thor said nothing; he just smiled, proudly shrugging at the entertainment he provided.

"Well, would you looky there. I knew she dyed them eyebrows blonde," the lady with the four teeny boobs on her back said, elbowing a fellow Little Rockette.

"Charlie, it was an accident. We need to go now," the drenched wife said, now posed with her hand over her crotch like the chick in Botticelli's painting, the *Birth of Venus*, except with hairspray matted hair and *Clockwork Orange* mascara. I followed them outside, mesmerized by the wet dress clinging to her moonscaped butt, and ducked behind the shrubs planted in front of the columns to leave my parting gift.

# Chapter 20

# Do Or Die

Things were bad. Real bad. Alice was gone. I'd seen nearly half the office with their pants down, and they weren't renewing my draw. I had 175 bucks to my name.

"We're not firing you, Jack. We just can't pay you anymore. You understand."

I did understand, but there were plenty of people like evil Debra they supported for a few extra months. That was all it would take to keep me from proving Mrs. Pohlkiss right. I knew it.

I dreaded going back to my studio. It smelled. The traffic was loud on the boulevard, and it was getting dirty. My rent was due and my landlady Hazel was hammering me to pay her. I even tried Mrs. Manchester for a loan, but she wouldn't return my phone calls. Dexter said she blamed me for his leaving.

I pulled up to the curb in front of my studio, and hadn't even turned off the Jeep, when Hazel appeared, holding her constant cocktail, brushing her frizzy dyed brown hair from her face. I heard she was forty-eight, but she looked sixty-five.

"You're two days late, Jackie."

"I know, I know. Could I just give you seventy-five dollars now?"

"You know the rules."

"Please, Hazel? I'm this close."

I held up two pinched fingers and looked at her through them.

"Sorry, baby. Gas, grass, or ass."

She followed at my heels, and then came inside my studio, spinning her large key ring around her index finger like a cocky lifeguard. I sunk down on my plaid couch and looked up at her, her beer belly suspended by her diagonally striped black and turquoise nylon dress. Could I? No. I just couldn't. My eyes rose to meet hers.

"You know I don't bite, Jackie." She held out her hand. I took it. What was I doing?

"My place is more comfortable," she said, leading me next door. I followed. Maybe when we got back to her place, we could just talk. She'd feel sorry for me.

I looked around the street to see if anyone was watching. She closed the door to her one-bedroom hippie pad behind us and twirled her front blinds closed, turning on a purple lava lamp.

"Need a drink, baby? Loosen things up?" she asked.

I was pretty certain things on her didn't need any more loosening up. She poured us two large doses of Old Crow from a half gallon into cloudy glasses. She offered me mine and held her drink next to the left cheek of her shrunken apple head complexion, and smiled. I drank mine down in one gulp, shuddering at more than just the sting of the booze. She savored hers while she swayed by the turntable.

"A little music ought to put us in the mood," she said, cranking Iron Butterfly.

"Shouldn't we talk first?" I yelled over the music.

"Talk won't pay the rent."

Hazel pulled me up to her and held me. I rested my head on her shoulder and closed my eyes, trying to think of something sexy. She was making it impossible.

"They're singing about the Garden of Eden in this song, but the singer was too drunk to say it right," she laughed and smiled.

I pushed her back a bit, but she clutched me even closer.

"Come on. I can't do all the work," she said.

Alain or Hazel, which was worse? It was the end of the line. I had no choice. No one could ever know. I was breaking my code. Selling out. She pulled my face to hers until we danced cheek to cheek.

I imagined I was back in high school with my prom date, Lindsey. She loved '70s rock too, and even had the same frizzy hair once from a home perm gone awry. Just thinking of Lindsey, I got a hard-on. It was a miracle from the Baby Jesus.

Some memories might fade, but STDs never would. I needed protection.

"I'll be right back." I rushed to the bathroom, furious that my body betrayed me with a woodie. I locked the door behind me and sifted through my wallet for my emergency rubber. It was gone! I opened the medicine cabinet for her stash, but there was nothing but toothpaste and Summer's Eve. I spied a tiny window above the bathtub. It was too small to escape through. My only shield from her hung on the shower curtain rod like a dead Jellyfish.

I grabbed the shower cap off the rod and charged out to battle.

"What's that for?" she asked.

"Protection."

"Mmm, I do love a man who's resourceful."

She pulled me down to the floor and kissed me with her hot gooey mouth, hiking up her dress before pulling down her full-sized panties.

I did my best not to look down and laid the cap over the general area, catching a glimpse of her untamed graying bush. Then I got down to work, gasping for breath between pumps to avoid smelling her patchouli oil.

I'm not sure who faked their orgasm first, but thankfully it was over quickly. I felt dirty—dirtier than when I stole eight Christmas trees from the chain link lot in front of Rosauers kind of dirty. I was able to toss the trees back over the fence the next night to erase the guilt back then, but this guilt was for keeps.

"We good?" I pleaded.

"Whoo!" She spanked my bare butt. "For a few weeks, I suppose."

I pulled my jeans up and ran out the door. I could make more money on Hollywood Boulevard. I would do a trade in three weeks or become homeless. It was that simple.

# Chapter 21

# Saved by Elvis

At work the next day, everyone's stares made me feel like they knew about Hazel. In my shame, I kept my head down and did nothing but call clients, which, after all, was my job.

"You sell them STRIP things?" a prospect in Greensboro twanged.

"Yes, sir. How many would you like?" I said. As if they were pizza slices.

"Oh, I think about a million or so, out round five years." This was it! I could feel it. I was about to be the man. I could barely breathe.

"You're done!" I blurted.

"Well, son. That was sure quick. What about the price?"

I covered the phone and flailed my arm at Phil to save me. Phil was my new favorite trader from Mississippi who could do an imitation of Elvis so well it was as if the King himself was in front of you. Now that Alice was gone, he was the only person who remotely gave a shit about me.

Phil ran over and grabbed the phone.

"Yes, sir. We're just securing the transaction here." Phil put his index finger over my mouth. "Exactly, sir. Everything is delivery versus payment. If this trade isn't exactly what we agreed upon, you pay nothing."

Phil nodded at me. I tried to speak, but he pinched my lips together.

"Do you have a pen, sir? Write this down. The total amount you'll be wiring us is," Phil continued on, adding numbers instantly in his head, leaving so much wiggle room in the price we could have completed the trade even if the United States declared war. Phil hung up and high-fived me. I stared in awe at my hero. He just made me $5,000 for two minutes of work. I couldn't stop staring and smiling at him.

"Stop. You're embarrassing me." Phil said. "I already know I'm a god. You should be doing ten of those a day." He walked back to his desk to avoid more gushing, leaving me to dream about all the future cars I could put an alarm on.

A moment later, still basking in my fog, Phil snuck up behind me. He grabbed my tie and jerked it up like a noose before cutting it. It was truly an honor.

"Ladies and gentlemen, a round of applause." Phil bellowed, holding my tie high in the air like a circus ringmaster. No one clapped. I knew their jealousy and rage firsthand.

Keri, the lone woman trader, rolled her eyes at me and mumbled something into her phone mouthpiece. Phil told me she was single and thirty-nine.

"It's the end of the line for her. She's gonna have to start fucking really old guys now. That's why she's been kind of bitchy lately," Phil explained.

Keri had thick bleached blonde hair that she tamed with a headband before it plunged down to her butt like a nun's wimple made of straw. It was clear someone must have told her how pretty her hair looked once too often as a child because she was still making it the focal point of her existence.

Right now, I longed for one of Alice's back rubs. I still had no friends, so I took Ron's cue and called *my* mom to tell her the good news. She wasn't home. Just like a lot of things, success was no fun unless you had someone to share it with.

## Chapter 22

# A New Beginning

The next day at work, people started treating me differently. Not as though they knew about Hazel or anything, but like I had something on them instead. At first I thought it was because they'd found out I'd seen them all naked in the owner's pool, but then I looked up on the leader board. There I was in all my magic marker glory. J. Fitzpatrick. Number ten out of ten because of that STRIP trade. I couldn't take my eyes off it. All I needed was just a few more of these accounts that traded these STRIP things, and then everyone would be kissing my ass like they should have been in the first place. I could be a lot of help to my coworkers, giving them a dose of cool, if they would just listen to me.

Most of the larger accounts were already taken, or hogged by the producers on their "protected" list. That way you couldn't shame them by opening the account when they were unable to. Not that it mattered most of the time. The huge accounts usually told us to get lost after our first call: our net capital was barely a million dollars.

"Y'all ain't big enough to sue if something goes in the shitter, or we make a trading mistake, and you need to fix it," explained the treasurer of a large city in the Midwest known for its wind and hot dogs.

Freedom decided a new company brochure could help combat this often-heard fear as well as bolster our image, which was weakening with every twang.

"I want everyone in their best get-ups tomorrow," Rick commanded.

The next morning was like grade school picture day. I popped into the bathroom for a quick pee and snuck past five producers jockeying for a spot in the only mirror, wetting down their hair, shamelessly deciding which fake smile looked best. How anyone who put forth so much effort could look worse than they normally did was astonishing, but these guys did.

The producers got a special perk of a take-home portrait because of their status. This created such a buzz you might have thought Ansel Adams was back from the dead and waiting in the kitchen.

I tried to appear unbothered that I wasn't receiving a portrait. The ex-receptionist, the one who I caught boning the owner—whose name I still can't remember—passed around a mock brochure that showed how the lucky few might appear if they were chosen to grace its pages. I prayed I wouldn't be chosen.

"All trades are fully disclosed by Prudential Bache," the front page proclaimed, specially wording it to sound like we were Pru's preferred bond specialist. The truth was we only hired them to process our trade tickets.

While the photographer roamed the room looking for candid shots, Trader Rick casually tried to be in the background of all of them with his chosen fake smile, posing with his arm on one hip like an underwear model in a glossy Sunday paper ad.

Keri was less inconspicuous. Today her hair was specially shellacked to shine like a maple cabinet. She struck a patient pose. Her cheeks sucked in, cradling the phone in her neck as she waited for a good twenty minutes while gazing down at her compact mirror for just the right facial expression she deemed made her look best. Nothing but her eyes moved which followed the photographer.

Eventually she tired of this and rubbed her cramped jaw joints with both hands. Finally the photographer headed her way, forcing her into a last-minute attention grabbing posture.

"You got some bubble gum on your shirt, Keri," Rick yelled across the floor. Keri looked down and covered up the top part of her exposed left aureole. Rick wasn't trying to be mean; he was just buying time to race over to be in the picture.

Neither Keri nor Rick would back down from wanting their picture taken. The photographer finally agreed on a G-rated group shot of them, standing underneath the five round clocks that showed what time it was in select major cities around the world, including Irvine.

But this gave me an idea. Instead of calling big cities, with big rules, why not call small places, with teeny-tiny rules—maybe even a city that understood gambling? Because after all, that's what investing really is. Some bets were just safer than others.

"Hello, Directory Assistance," I whispered. "I need the city offices for South Lake Tahoe."

I tracked down the portfolio manager an hour later at his main job running the Pig in a Poke rib joint.

"Now, who are you?" the man asked.

"Jack Fitzpatrick. I sell government securities."

"I've never had one of these phone calls before."

I wanted to sing like a lady soprano hitting a high note in church choir.

"We've only got a million dollars in the whole reserve fund," he said.

"At least that's something, sir!" This fact would keep them far away from any sane broker's call list and allow me time to build my manipulation—I mean, sales—skills.

I called him every day at the rib joint for a month, just after his lunch rush so he would be a little exhausted and harried. Every day I hoped was the day I could "pull his pants down," as the term came to be known once a client agreed to do trades with you.

That fateful pantsing day arrived a mere four weeks later.

"How much will $200,000 buy me?" he asked.

"About a million dollars face, sir, if we do the thirty-year STRIP."

The further out the bond, the more risk. Also, the more money the broker can hide in a trade. To put it in perspective, the difference between 10 percent and 10.07 percent on a million-dollar bond out thirty years was worth $10,000. But on a bond that matured in a year, that same difference was only $70. Time really was money.

"Get me some prices and get back to me after lunch," South Lake said.

Debra sidled up to me as I hung up the phone. I greedily rubbed my hands together.

"You know, I had an idea to call South Lake too."

"It's on my protected list." I stood up.

"I know; I just checked."

"It's not polite to eavesdrop."

"Jack, you know California cities can't buy securities out past five years."

Debra looked down at my notebook while I moved my arm over the page.

"You know, Debra, I was going to give you the city of Lompoc. The guy says he only trusts women."

I tore Lompoc's contact sheet out of my account book and handed it to her.

"Sounds like you're both smart men." Debra nodded and walked away. Lompoc was a pain in my ass: the finance director was going through a nasty divorce. He and Debra were perfect for each other.

I needed this South Lake trade bad. If my buyer knew Hazel, he'd have probably given me $500,000 to spend. Fuck my conscience. I pretended, just like all the producers who bought bonds maturing past five years for their California cities, that I was unaware and bought the gambling city its first STRIP. Now I was no better than the rest of the sleazebags. I had done it, and there was no turning back. It was *South* Lake Tahoe after all, I assured myself, hoping this little infraction wouldn't come back to haunt me.

I felt guilty the entire drive home. It brought me back to the first time I masturbated: I promised myself I'd never do it again. Of course, it didn't work then, and it wasn't going to work now, either. I compromised with myself to at least not overtrade the account, whatever that meant.

For this to happen, I needed a nice stable of about ten more of these dirty little hamlets. Then I could be a full-fledged bond daddy, and easily maintain my new respect at the office.

Combing Gold Country for small towns was easy, but educating them was excruciating, and relaxing them enough to do a trade was downright embarrassing.

"I've never done this before," stammered the treasurer of Grass Valley.

"There, there now. This might hurt a little bit at first," I said, just before executing their first long bond trade.

Unfortunately, interest rates crept up for the next two weeks, bond prices went down, and all my STRIP customers got scared, including me.

"My boss isn't going to take kindly to this if I'm stuck in this bond for thirty years," Nevada City said.

"But you won't be at your job for thirty years, sir."

"I'll be dead next week if you don't make this right," he insisted.

"We can always sell them if we need to."

"I told you, I can't take a loss."

"Don't think of it as a loss. Think about it like you just made less than you would have if you left it in the bank."

None of my customers liked that last line, and I was left with no trades for two weeks. That's when Wyatt wiped my name off the leader board, after he made sure I was watching.

But almost as soon as Wyatt put down the eraser, a news flash jumped on the Telerate screen. Unemployment was up more than expected! Bad news in the bond market created a frenzy, like escaped reform school boys flipping over an ice cream truck.

"We're rocking and rolling," Rick yelled, prompting his trademark Chubby Checker impersonation of the twist, drying off his ass with an imaginary towel. "I can feel my bonus growing by the minute!" he glowed, staring at the florescent lights.

That morning, interest rates fell, and prices went up just enough to where I could make $3,000 commission and South Lake could make $1,000 profit.

"Rates will be back up next week. We can buy them cheaper if we sell now," I said, like I meant it.

All my customers agreed, and that was it. That was all I had to do. I finally had a plan, my niche. But I wasn't home free yet. There were still plenty of new distractions to keep me from my fortune.

# Chapter 23

# Finally Some Friends

Freedom had two new hires: Arthur, a six-feet-five, 280-pound black man with a voice like Barry White; and Manny, a nice college-educated Jewish kid from Manhattan who decided to stay in LA after graduating from Occidental. Manny was someone I knew I could finally be friends with at work after I noticed the restrained horror on his face as he was introduced around the floor. I also had never had a Jewish friend before, and I was curious to see what all the hype was about.

Arthur and Manny developed a solid bond during their training video week, just like Alice and me, but unlike us, they went to happy hour together. I was jealous until one Friday I finally got an invite.

We arrived at a local Mexican Cantina and joined two scraggly backpacker girls from Australia who invited us to sit at their table for their third round of "kick-ass" margaritas.

"Whose tits do you think are biggah?" said the brown-haired one, Nandalia.

I was the first to accept their invitation to squeeze the Charmin, followed by Arthur and Manny. Everyone had a different opinion, so we had to play again.

"Umm, you guys are going to have to leave," our flat-chested waitress insisted, with her manager standing cross-armed behind her.

Now, I hadn't fallen off the turnip truck yesterday, but when the five of us piled into Arthur's maroon Cadillac El Dorado, I thought we were just going somewhere else for drinks, and maybe, at its nastiest, some more groping at the next bar. Arthur could be our father, for Chrissakes.

But then we walked into Arthur's living room at a sprawling two-level apartment complex. The lights stayed off, except for a mood light in the corner. Arthur pushed a button, and Marvin Gaye started singing. I got kind of scared. The scars from Hazel were far from healed.

Arthur didn't even bother to take the backpack off the one named Sheila. He pulled her pants straight down to her ankles. She took eager baby steps toward where Arthur was sitting naked on the couch. Any stray skid marks wouldn't matter on his torn-up leather model.

I turned my head to Manny, hoping he would be in shock too, but he was already writhing with Nandalia on the carpet.

"Holy hell, what is that smell?!" Manny said, fanning his hand in front of his face. His look of disgust was illuminated by the stereo.

"Sorry, mate. It's been a tough month on the road," Nandalia said, pulling her underwear back up.

I slipped deeper into the safety of the kitchen shadows and lay still against the wall, hoping they would forget I was there.

"Jack, get me some of that whipping cream out the fridge."

My panic reignited. I started for the front door, but it was blocked by bodies. There was no back door. I patted my pockets. No cash for a cab. I was too drunk to steal Arthur's car.

I opened the nearly empty fridge and grabbed the Reddi Whip. I lobbed it underhanded in Arthur's general direction like a softball.

"Catch!" I said.

The can smacked Sheila on the ear.

"Ow!" Sheila rubbed her head.

Arthur quieted her down by spraying her breasts with the aerated vegetable oil. I crawled under the kitchen table to hide, pulling the chairs in front of me to lock myself in. The foot of the table became my pillow. I passed out dead until a painful crick in my neck forced me awake. I heard the comforting, loud rumble of Arthur's snore. Finally safe. It was over. But a few moments later, I heard a few quick snorts.

"Hey, that's mine." Arthur said, struggling up from the couch.

I peered through the chair legs. Sheila was riding on top of Manny while Nandalia was passed out next to them. She was naked, save for her panties. Arthur stood up; his horse-sized penis flopped midthigh. He lifted Sheila off Manny, making a popping noise, like when you thrust your thumb out of your mouth. Manny was too tired to argue as Arthur carried her back into his bedroom.

I laid my head back down and sucked my thumb, repeating to myself, "There's no place like home; there's no place like home," until I passed out again.

"Zip-uh-dee-doo-dah, zip-uh-dee-aye."

I peered up from under the table, squinting in the morning sun. Arthur was singing. He stood in front of the stove, his stained tighty-whities covered by an apron, while the other three eagerly held their plates behind him, jostling from one leg to the other.

"Come on, Jack, get ya sef some pancakes and eggs."

Old people sure know how to charge through their hangovers. Arthur rocked back on his heels waiting for the eggs to cook, holding a red spatula. Arthur had no shame from last night. He was casual, like it was Sunday breakfast at Grandma's house. I almost believed it, except for his braless man boobs.

## Chapter 24

# If You're Gonna Do Something, Do It Right

"Jack, what does it mean when you guys say, 'No talking, goddamnit,' and then laugh?" Mr. Lincoln cornered me at the water cooler, his blank expression demanding an answer. I had no choice but to confide to him our running joke about the training tapes. So in a way, Darwin getting hired was all my fault.

Darwin was from Arkansas, of course. He was hired not only to whip the newbies into shape but also to teach the secrets of success to the 80 percent of the sales force who were barely making the draw.

"Salespeople, like sales itself, is a numbers game," Darwin explained to the owners, who stood at the rear of the trading floor with their arms crossed, nodding out to their flock.

They shook hands and gave Darwin the okay to hire as many freaks as possible, even lining the hallways with new desks.

Darwin took over the glossy table in the conference room as his headquarters and called his new trainees the "Talking Heads." He taught them how to cold call, how to overcome objections, how to gain trust, and, most importantly, how to get control of clients and pull their pants down. When Darwin decided you were ready to leave the playpen for the real trading floor, you got to walk to the front of the room and ceremoniously pull down the pants of a two foot Chucky doll dressed in a three-piece suit, just to remind you what you were here for.

"Go get 'em, tiger!"

"Hooray!" the room would yell to the lucky graduate.

# Chapter 25

# Fair and Fair Alike

Darwin worked a deal with the owners for a cut of the federal tax credits for hiring disabled people and minorities. So he was especially elated when he hired an obese man in a wheelchair named Ira Berkowitz.

"I got me a double-bagger-for-real Talking Head this time!" Darwin boasted, patting Ira on the back.

Darwin became a little dismayed, however. He had to drop the double-bagger part: Jews weren't considered minorities outside of Arkansas.

"Don't you worry, Ira. We're gonna make your little predicament work for us," Darwin said, patting Ira's atrophied legs.

"I want you mentioning your chair on every call. Take your anger out on them, like it's their fault. I'm planning my trip to Hawaii on you."

I watched Ira in action.

"Aren't state-run organizations required to do business with disabled people?" Ira said to anyone about to hang up on him.

It worked like flipping a switch. In two weeks, that lucky fucker shot past me on the leader board.

Now everyone wanted their own special flavor of bullshit to get easy business.

"I'm part Indian," someone as white as me claimed to a cold call.

Then Kurt Michaels and Rob Trapper realized they were disabled veterans and would qualify too. One had a busted knee from playing football at Army, and one had a shell in his eye listed on his medical record—an eggshell, that is, from a food fight in the mess hall.

This client-catching trick soon swept all over Wall Street, and the regulators had to step in. Now to legitimately force the issue, these brokers had to become an "official" Disabled Veteran's Enterprise. After that, they would be allowed in all state municipal underwritings, and the big customers would be forced by law to direct a percentage of their total order flow to them, resulting in sales credits ranging from $2,500 to as much as $10,000 per million, regardless of the firm's measly capital. This loophole was soon extended to women and other minorities.

It was all bullshit. What about me, the white boy from Spokane? I was the only one like me on the floor, and I wasn't benefitting from this crap at all. Isn't half the population of the world female? And way less than half of California white?! The original plan was supposed to force some power away from the White Boy Network dominating Wall Street, but I wasn't part of their tribe anyway.

To qualify for this preferred status, 51 percent of the firm needed to be owned by a minority. Within the year, hundreds of white able-bodied brokers left their large firms all over the country to start their own boutique firms with minority figureheads they found on the street, and the street wasn't "Wall" Street.

"Jack, how would you like to give a fella a hand? I can't keep up with all this business," Kurt said to me as I fumed with my arms crossed. "I just take 5 percent." They were able to open their boutique firm underneath the umbrella of Freedom Capital and not have to leave the office.

I was no longer Mr. Bitterman. All the big banks that told me to go pound sand just a month before were now required to do business because I worked for a Disabled Veteran Enterprise. A few of them were even happy, since now they wouldn't get shut out of the limited supply of new deals.

As long as I had my cake, I would sit in my corner and pig out and make my fuck-you money, even though I knew in my heart, this way of thinking had ruined far greater empires than the one I was trying to build.

# Chapter 26

# Girls, Girls, Girls

"You fellers ain't gonna let a woman make more money than you?" Darwin said, introducing his newest addition, six-feet-two blonde Marilyn fresh back from Germany. I thought for a moment I recognized her. Was it from a drugstore package of those "Big Mama" pantyhose? Where there was a photo on the label of three very large women wearing nothing but pantyhose, turned to the side so you couldn't see their beavers while they held their huge knockers in one arm? It wasn't her. I asked.

Marilyn was very excited as she unpacked all her things, dumping the contents of a cardboard box straight into a file cabinet. It was time to try to shine some of my new light.

"So, how is it being back in the States?"

"I didn't want to come back."

"Well, why did you?" I asked.

"The father of my son called Immigration on me."

"At least you got a job."

"I didn't want to, but Mom and Dad said I had to get out of the house during the day because I talk too much."

"How lucky." My internal light flickered, but after all, she was a fresh new freak to mesmerize me while I trudged through my cold calling. But even that was soon clouded when I found out she had a flatulence problem.

"It must be the red meat," she shrugged, after I could no longer be polite and took to waving a manila folder at her after each onslaught.

The next week, her little boy came to visit Mommy at work. He looked just like the blond chubster who fell in the chocolate river at Willy Wonka's factory. It was heartwarming to see him dash up for a hug, until he poked at Marilyn's boob and said, "Nook, nook."

Without a word, she whipped out her rugby football-sized tit and gave the young man a snack right there in front of me, his face disappearing in her flesh. Wasn't it just yesterday she told me he was five and a half years old and that he could read?! I told myself to act cool and natural. Get over it, you prude. Just because I had never seen this doesn't mean it wasn't totally fine. I was better, until she leaned back, closed her eyes, and let out a little moan while she petted his hair.

"Don't you think it's time to knock him off the tit? I mean, your snack bar won't be so handy when school starts next year."

"I don't think that's going to happen." She patted the back of my hand. Silly me. "My new boyfriend likes to drink it too."

That's when it finally hit me, like a shot of breast milk in the eye. They would hire just about anyone that walked in the door.

But it's not fair to say everyone they hired was a bumbling boob. Some good ones slipped through the cracks and failed. After Marilyn, there was Jeannette. She was sharp and quick-witted like Alice, and sported merely B cups.

"Jack, I've got nobody's pants to pull down," she confided in me, her draw nearing its end.

I hugged her protectively, because just like in the wild, once there was evidence you were going to die, the hyenas would step in to torment you in the final hours. The leader of Freedom's hyena pack was named Trusack.

"Hey, Jeannette, I'll buy you a turkey sandwich if you give me City of Fresno now. It'll be mine in a few weeks anyway." He jeered, looking out the window to a tow truck repo-ing her Buick Skylark from the parking garage.

"Look on the bright side, Jeannette. It can't get much worse than this, can it?" I asked.

"Yeah, I guess I could end up giving Trusack a blowjob in the parking garage, right?" She laughed, but I saw tears in her eyes.

"Don't worry. I can run you home tonight," I offered.

"Thanks."

We hugged again.

At the end of the next day, after I'd left, Jeanette was fired. And in the quiet of the late afternoon while she was miserably cleaning out her desk, Trusack convinced her to go to the parking garage. He got his blowjob.

"Sorry, Jack. I really needed to hit rock bottom before I could dust myself off," she explained when I called her the next morning to see if Trusack was spreading lies.

That wasn't rock bottom; that was 20,000 leagues under the sea.

"Well, he gave me a ride home," she justified.

# Chapter 27

# Learn to Take It Like a Man

I was beginning to mature, a little bit. Not like I was ready to volunteer at an orphanage or anything. I don't even know if you could call it compassion, but I was learning to accept the freaks as best I could, and ignore the hyenas. But the one thing I could not ignore was the trading desk. No trader meant no trades, which meant no business, which meant giving Trusack a blowjob in the parking garage. I shuddered. Unless you were a producer, you had to fight twice as hard for the attention of the gang of traders. Fat Wyatt had the best street contacts, and he wouldn't share them with you unless you got your tongue way up his ass. Then there was Keri, who hated me more than ever since I was producing. You see, she used to be in sales but failed. Then, of course, there was—thank you, God—my savior. Phil.

My new kinder, gentler self was feeling good with Phil guiding my light until the inevitable came. Phil went on vacation. The week he was gone I made it until Friday, using the time to cold call until the STRIP-buying guy from Greensboro called.

"Jack, give me some late '09 Treasury levels."

I stood up and caught Keri's eye. She walked off, leaving me no choice but to walk up and politely wait for Wyatt to finish with another salesman.

Why did he have to be sporting the most ginormous zit I've ever seen in my life on his forehead? I couldn't take my eyes off it. It was obviously on his mind too, because the moment the other salesman left, he proceeded to pop the pink volcano like I wasn't even there. I grimaced. He held his breath and pushed his left index finger on one side of this third eye, then wrapped his other arm over the top of his head so the opposing finger could give weighted leverage for a clean squeeze. I guess he figured after shitting in his shoe in front of me, this would be nothing for me to watch.

Experience told me just to slip away and leave him to his private moment, but I needed these prices now! And maybe this was finally my chance to make friends with the enemy. I could pretend it was no big deal. We all get zits. Well, maybe ones that aren't the size of Volkswagens, but still.

"Wyatt, could I please get a bid on two million 0-9 callable zits—uh STRIPS,-please?" I did my best to avoid looking straight at him, but also made sure I was out of firing range, in case his zit exploded.

He ignored me, and grunted and pushed full force like he was taking a shit, letting out a loud anguished sigh. The zit had popped underneath the skin and it was clearly painful. He looked me dead in the eye; folded his hands; peered around to make sure no one was in earshot and beckoned me. My eyes got big. I knew what was coming. He was going to take the pain of his zit out on me!

"Listen to me, you little sonuvabitch. You think you can just buddy-buddy up with Phil, and ignore me? Make me look like shit."

"You're so busy, sir. You're the top."

"Don't patronize me. I'm the one in charge."

"Of everyone. I know, I know."

"You have to worship me until I decide you're worthy."

"How am I doing?"

He narrowed his eyes at me. Shit.

"Listen to me. I'm going to do everything in my power to make you fail, and if you tell anyone, I'm just gonna deny it."

"But why?" I whimpered.

"Because you remind me of the guy who fucked my wife back in Boston."

"It wasn't me," I protested.

"Get out of my face."

I ambled back in a daze. It was all too much. I was paying the price for his horny ex-wife twenty-five states away. I couldn't sell bonds unless I had prices, and if I told the owners, they'd think I was crazy and fire me for sure. There was no trader left to get prices from.

My lower lip buckled. I had the sensation of uncontrollable tears I hadn't felt since I was a toddler. I was having a meltdown. Cracking up. If I cried in front of anyone, I was doomed. I slammed open the side door to the emergency stairwell and headed down to the safety of my trusty Jeep. I reclined the bucket seat to hide from the world and wailed like a baby. I wanted to quit, but I would rather die than give Mrs. Pohlkiss, and every other asshole, just what they wanted.

After twenty minutes I sat up, blew my nose on my shirttail and drove home. Mother Fate wasn't telling me to move on this time. She was telling me to quit being a pussy.

# Chapter 28

# Rough and Ready

If I had to be miserable here, someone—or a lot of someones—were going to pay for what I was going through.

Bring on the freaks! No one they could hire would distract me from my goal anymore. Not even the flashy new guy named Nadar, who wore silk shirts and Tom Jones polyester pants that made his package look enormous. His hairy chest was ornamented with gold chains.

Word traveled fast about Nadar's background. Just a month ago, he arrived home at his deluxe house on Lido Island, and found his wife of twenty-three years hanging from a jump rope in her workout Lycra with an empty bottle of sleeping pills and a bottle of Jack Daniels nearby. She didn't drink. His twenty-one-year-old son, Nadar Junior, arrived home to find his hysterical father kicking chairs around the room with his mother still slowly swinging. Those in the know said it was because he wouldn't give her a divorce.

Freedom hired his son, Nadar Junior, a week after they brought Nadar on board. Unlike the normal newbie torture the office heaped on everyone, Nadar Junior got a break after this awful story, even from Wyatt.

Junior was actually pretty cool and invited Manny, Arthur, and me over to his dad's house for some beers after work. It felt good to make him laugh, even though he sometimes would stop himself during a deep guffaw, feeling it wasn't yet time to forget his mother.

We were having a great time until Nadar Senior came home hammered, with a twenty-two-year-old blonde bimbette, who he shoved straight into his bedroom. We all felt bad for Junior, so we were careful only to eavesdrop at the bedroom door when Junior was in the kitchen.

Then, the bedroom door swung open. The young girl pushed us aside and fled. Senior sauntered out with his hands on his hips, clad only in a towel and a big fat smile.

"I shaved her cookie as bald as a ping pong ball," he boasted, forcing obligatory high-fives from us. His towel crumpled to the carpet.

The look on Junior's face was beyond sadness as his naked father slapped him on the back and sauntered back to his room, closing the door on our view of his hairy back and saggy butt.

Maybe my situation wasn't so bad after all. Junior had nowhere to go, either. Dads that were still alive might not be all they were cracked up to be. Although I was pretty sure that if my dad was still alive he wouldn't be shaving the neighbor girls. But I'd never know the difference. Even though I'd love to have a dad, even one that embarrassed me, I'd have to quit feeling sorry for myself. No one owed me or anybody else anything. My life was easy to most of the world.

# Chapter 29

# The Secret

Nadar was different than the rest of the freaks. He wasn't disabled or a minority. He just did business. He shot up the leader board within weeks. By watching and listening to him, he finally revealed to me the big secret of the producers.

Service, schmervice. We were here to make as much money as possible without the customer finding out how much they were overpaying. That part wasn't the secret. The secret was how you did it.

It went like this. If someone gave you a hard time about a price, or put you in too much competition, you narrowed your profit margin to next to nothing to win that trade. That way if they didn't give you the business you'd know you were wasting your time; they were just using you to price their real brokers. But if you did win, you'd do that a couple more times until finally you were their pet dove. Then you could viciously punish them with a huge mark when you knew they were too busy and not checking other dealers' offers since they thought you were the low-price leader.

Kind of like grocery store ads for cheap hamburger that get you in the door so they can really stick it to you with overpriced light bulbs and raspberries. You were in the store already and just wanted to get the hell out of there.

"It's just good clean business, Jack. Hard work mixed with talent," Thor used to say when I first asked him for his tricks of the trade. Now I knew why they said nothing. It was so simple, so dirty. Anybody could do it.

Getting the guts up to try it was nerve-wracking. I needed every penny to avoid the clutches of Hazel or a permanent trip back to Spokane. But the next week I held my breath and worked for free, and my trades doubled. Now they were starting to owe me. It was time for some serious pants pulling.

"Atta boy, Jack. I told you, ya need a little larceny in your heart to be good at this." Phil rubbed my shoulders as I filled out an $8,000 commission ticket. I looked up to Wyatt and winked. That was probably a mistake, but even he couldn't stop me. The next week I made $25,000. Then only $3,000, but the following week netted me $30,000.

"I think you're ready for the big time," Phil said as I looked up at him like a puppy from my chair.

"What could be better than this?" I asked.

"A little I-O-P-O action," he whispered.

It was as filthy and scary as the word heroin. They were derivatives, a word only to be mentioned under your breath. Not even the traders at Merrill knew what they were really worth.

"You serious? I don't know. Those things are kind of tricky, aren't they?"

Phil leaned in closer. "All you need to know is, if your customer thinks rates are going up, you sell them an I-O. And if they think they are going down?"

"A P-O."

"See! You don't need to convince them. Let them fill in the blanks. The customers are always right."

"What if they think rates are going to stay the same?"

"You sell them both!"

The letters stood for interest only and principal only, and if you put them together you would have a mortgage bond. "Theoretically," Phil said. "That's what you tell them anyway. It's just like the one they pay every month, only with several points missing to our fine industry."

Phil printed out yield charts for us to fax, detailing the huge returns, which were based on how fast the mortgage pools had been paying down or refinancing their loans. This was known as their PSA speed—not the antigen test they give for your prostate, but somewhat similar. Customers were indeed getting these bonds shoved up their asses.

The faxing part was easy and allowed me to trick myself into thinking I was being useful, planting seeds for harvest, until Phil stood behind me.

"Don't be afraid, boy! You're going about it all wrong."

"But I freeze up when they ask me to explain what the fuck they are," I said.

"Don't worry about that part. Get friendly."

"I've got my nose so far up their ass I can barely breathe," I complained.

"Not you. You gotta make the securities sound friendly. Start by calling them by their fun names: Ginnie Mae, Fannie Mae, and Freddy Mac. Make them feel like they're joining a club with their down-home neighbor."

"But I told you, I don't even understand it!"

"That's fine. Most of them are dumber than dirt. Plus you can believe in it more this way. You think soldiers would fight if they really knew what they were fighting for?"

That hurt. My dad knew plenty.

"Remember the first time you got high?"

"Sure."

"Everyone else was doing it, and you wanted to be cool."

"They're still not gonna give me a million dollars so they can be cool."

"They will with these," Phil scruffed six concert tickets under my chin.

"So I take them out; we become friends and—"

"No, dummy. You just give these to them. They don't want to hang out with you, either."

I examined the tickets—home plate seats to the Dodgers and two front row seats to Madonna at the Forum.

"Then you've got something to hang over their heads if they start bitching," Phil said.

"Bitching about what?"

"Rates going the wrong way; the instant big loss on their portfolio pricing because of your mystery commission. Lots of things."

"How come you aren't in sales?" I asked.

"I don't like feeling dirty," Phil said.

I knew all about feeling dirty. This was nothing compared to Alain or Hazel.

"Go get 'em, tiger. My bonus needs you." Phil squeezed my shoulders till they hurt.

"But can't these I-O things be worthless overnight?"

"Jack. Tell me one thing."

"One thing," I said.

"Whoever told you Freedom Fucking Capital Markets was a branch of the Red Cross?"

He was right. This wasn't charity work.

Phil was so successful convincing the rest of the office on these I-O things that Freedom had to buy three new fax machines. Darwin even added a new training section for producers on these mysterious securities.

But there was only so much talent to pull from Orange County, and the quality of hires diminished with each plopped-down legal pad. The pact I'd made to stay focused was becoming nearly impossible. The place was sounding like Foghorn Leghorn was visiting Petticoat Junction.

For instance, there was Darwin's latest hire, a dancer he met at Captain Cremes, a strip club in a strip mall out near the El Toro Marine Base. It was the fancier of the two strip clubs that shared a parking lot: the one next to Bob's 99 Cent Store, not the one wedged in the middle near the dildo shop.

Darwin had to remember to start calling her Beverly instead of Chanterelle. I wondered how fungus grown in shit was such a great stage name, but she didn't talk to me.

"Beverly's so bright she can speak in tongues," Darwin said to calm the concerned owners as he twinkled pet fingers at her. "And a big money day makes her purr louder than a lion ever could."

The owners had bigger fires to put out. They were getting sued by the state of New Mexico after the state found out that they paid way too much on a Treasury security that Freedom had sold them. Freedom's defense, just like every other brokerage firm that got sued, was "buyer beware." No one held a gun to their heads, and anyone running millions of dollars better know what they were doing.

Chanterelle didn't know anything about the bond business, but she knew plenty about pleasing the customer. Because of that, she was a natural to take charge of the upcoming thirtieth birthday of our fellow broker, Frank.

"Frank, Sheryl from Danville is here to see you," the receptionist announced. Frank was surprised that his new sugar momma client was visiting all the way from Northern California, but it wasn't out of the question. As the young woman approached, wearing a shirtless blue pin-striped suit, he jumped up to straighten his tie and stood at attention.

Frank blushed when the woman daintily presented her hand and moved her glasses down her nose at him. This was Beverly's cue to hit the play button on a giant boom box. Aerosmith's "Dude Looks Like a Lady" blared across the trading room floor, which instantly smelled of sex. The imposter bared it all down to her panties amid the hoots and hollers of the male majority.

I glanced up to the Irvine wall clock. It was twelve forty-five. Maybe being a stripper would be a more popular job if the hours were more civilized, like here in Orange County?

I had to get out of this place. I could do better. But I was making bank. I had made over $250,000 so far this year. After only two years, I'd made more than ten years' worth of work for the average Spokanite. Freedom was the only game in this town for bond brokers, and from what I could figure, I knew Wall Street was filled with pricks like Wyatt. It was time to check out the job market in San Francisco, not to mention getting a much-needed friend fix from Dexter. Even though we talked three times a week, I hadn't seen him in six months.

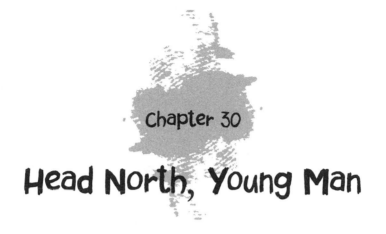

# Chapter 30

# Head North, Young Man

I exited the blue Super Shuttle Van in the Marina, took a long cool breath, and watched the foggy San Francisco sea breeze evaporate into the bright blue sky. It was a nice break from the year-round white sun of LA. For the first time since I started selling bonds, my head was free of the freaks.

I arrived at the address Dexter gave me and walked up the steep maroon painted front porch stairs of an old green house. A chubby disheveled guy wearing a plaid sport coat and a new-growth mustache opened the large wooden door. He was eating a taquito.

"Good, you're finally here," the man said. He had the same voice as Dexter and looked curiously familiar even though I was sure I'd never seen him before.

"What you looking at, you fuck?!" the man barked.

"Is Dexter here?"

The man hugged me.

"Get off me."

Just as I pushed him off, I recognized the tip of his nose. It was Dexter, fifty pounds heavier.

"What happened to you?"

"Food's a ripper up here," Dexter said, patting his new impressive gut.

"Wow, you're not kidding!"

"Plans have changed, mate. We're going up north on a float trip."

"A what?"

"You know, on a rivuh," he said, tossing the crusty end of the taquito behind him. He grabbed his wheeled bag and forced me backward down the porch stairs.

"Best behavior. All the bosses from the main office will be there."

"I didn't come up here to be on good behavior. And what is with your sport coat?"

"It's what top-ten-in-the-region Ricoh copier salesmen like myself wear for casual wear," he said.

Surely he hadn't sold out and become an ass kisser. I was speechless.

"Shut your hole. It'll all be free. You'll love it." He spun me around and stuffed me in his car.

The "free" part was good, but if these bosses didn't know the real Dexter by the end of the weekend, I would make sure they did.

# Chapter 31

# Scary Campfire Stories Are Not for Kids

The mood was perfect for a late summer car nap: sunny, the AC cranked, my socked feet propped up on the dash, and my best friend behind the wheel. I felt safe until my head started banging against the window. Dexter was squealing around the curves of the North Fork of the Yuba River.

"Wakey, wakey. Eggs and bakey."

Dexter slapped my cheek. He knew I hated that.

We pulled in at a campsite and parked between a red Ford Minivan and a beat-up '60s Dodge Dart with a Humboldt State bumper sticker spelled out with marijuana leaves.

"They beat us," he said.

I helped him unload the car and tried to think positively. We customized our tent with a beer-stocked Playmate cooler in one corner and a late-night pee jar in the other.

"Smoke a bowl, dude?" A shaggy teenager poked his head into our tent.

Maybe this wasn't going to be so bad after all. I glanced at fearful Dexter before leaving the canvas sanctuary.

"Dude, don't get all fucked up, and start telling my boss that his kid has great pot. I know you, man," Dexter growled after me as I headed into the raspberry bushes surrounding our tents.

Was I that bad? Well, maybe in the past, but he had no idea how much I had matured. These lonely months had made me into a man. And who was he to lecture me, anyway?

The raspberry thicket where we hid to smoke provided privacy and perfectly ripe nuggets of juicy refreshment to soothe our scorched throats between hits from his green plastic minibong.

Being from the Northwest, I'd smoked my fair share of pot, so I'm qualified to say that without a doubt that kid had the strongest pot ever. "Humboldt Crippler," he called it. I bounced off the vines on my way out of the labyrinth, not feeling a scratch, only the beauty in the congealing thin blood lines on my forearm.

Back in the tent, Dexter was happy I was incapacitated so I couldn't bother his bosses. He confidently zipped me up inside our tent so he could go out and brown-nose. My buzz lasted for hours, leaving me little choice but to lie back on my blow-up mattress and listen to the Cure on my Walkman while I made shadow animals with my hands against the glow of the deep orange sunset.

Nearing the end of my playtime, a large head with brown shoulder-length hair lurched in through the tent flap. My fingers were still wiggling.

"What are you doing in here? Don't be shy. It's campfire time!" The thing patted my legs. "It's gonna be just us chickens tonight. The rest of the group is driving up tomorrow."

The scary head was attached to Dexter's manager, Kathy. She was dressed in a cheap pink sweat suit and stood outside our tent, banging her hands together like the Energizer bunny, blinking at me through large round glasses until I stumbled outside to follow her.

When I joined Dexter around the campfire, the power I felt from his look of horror made me wish I'd cozied up around the fire sooner.

"What's up, me old Shem-wa?" I patted Dexter on the back and spun my lawn chair in between him and the teenaged son while Kathy nestled in across from us to complete our circle. That's when Dexter hit me in the chest for the first time.

"Quit smiling, dude. She's gonna know," Dexter said.

I hated it when he hit me, and even worse when I was baked, so I sat pouting like a high-maintenance girlfriend until the teenaged son cracked open a bottle of Jack Daniels and passed it to me. I smiled. Dexter knew something disastrous was about to happen.

Before I could even get my buzz on, Dexter kicked my chair and insisted, "Shape up!" He wouldn't let me smile. He wouldn't even let me pout. I was getting pissed. He had broken the camel's back.

I looked directly into his eyes. I wasn't doing a damn thing wrong. I'd show him shape up. That's when it all fell apart.

"I just love being in the great outdoors, hanging out around the campfire, being one of the guys," Kathy said, stoking the fire and looking dreamily at Dexter.

"Me too, Kath," Dexter smiled back at her with soft lips, his head cocked to the right.

I suppressed a moan and mimicked Dexter's gestures. Only when Kathy glanced away would Dexter punch me to stop.

"I've got an idea!" Kathy jumped up with the stick still in her hand. She reminded me of the time when Mrs. Pohlkiss tricked me into unclogging her sewer main with the handle of a broom. Pohlkiss sewage had splashed all over me.

"Let's tell scary stories!" Kathy perked.

I watched Dexter's eyes, still lovingly fixated on Kathy.

"Yeah? Well, I've got a scary story for you! Why don't we all throw you in the sticker bushes and fuck you?" I blurted.

A laugh, harder than I've ever tried to laugh, attempted to come out, but instead I fell over backward in my lawn chair, gasping for breath in tears. Crickets chirped. I felt so free, so happy. I'd finally told Mrs. P to fuck off.

Dexter wasn't sure what had happened, but with one look down at me with my feet still in the air, he started cackling too, for an uncomfortable length of time not suitable for any employee.

Kathy wasn't Mrs. Pohlkiss. Shit. What did I just do? She knew it was a joke, right? She walked right into it. I had to make quick reparations or it might be disastrous for my best friend.

"Kidding. Kidding. Sorry, sorry, sorry. How about a game of Indian?" I crawled over to her on my knees with true and honest intentions.

"I've never heard of that." Kathy was still angry but seemed pleased with the whole group game idea. She looked almost ready to forgive me, to save the evening.

"It's easy. Everyone has a name and a hand motion. You play it just like Thumper. If you fuck up, you drink."

"Thump her?" Kathy was alarmed; surely I was speaking in some kind of code.

"Yeah, you know, Thumper?" I wiggled my index finger at her like a swimming fish.

"Your boy Dexter there can be Shooting Sperm." I put my index fingers on either side of my head like feathers in a headband. "Dude with the whiskey, Kurt, gets to be Chief Jack 'Em Off, and you, my little lady, get to be Dripping Cunt." I twinkled my fingers in a downward motion like a waterfall.

Kathy threw her stick in the fire. Game over. Shit.

"That's the name the girls always fought for, wasn't it, Dexter?" I asked.

"I'm going to bed. *Alone!*" she fumed. She stomped into the darkness, glancing back to make sure we weren't going to hoist her over our heads and run like natives with her into the raspberry thicket.

"Wait! You can be Wong Woman! We can make up a new one, a nice one. Squaw of the Holy Goodness. Whatever you want."

It was too late. No sticker bushes or drinking games for Kathy. I had really done it now. I looked down at Dexter, still laughing, lying on his stomach while Kurt chanted, "Oooooga Chaka, Oooooga Chaka, Oooooga Chaka, Oooooga, ooogah!" sending Dexter into more fits.

I don't really remember going to bed, but the next morning the rest of the group, about seven of them, I was told, showed up. We were too hung over to float. Plus, they didn't wake us to join them.

We headed back early to the city. I wasn't sure if Dexter was mad at me or not. We didn't talk about it, and anyway I slept most of the drive back. It wasn't until my flight home that I started to feel really bad. My guilt lasted for about a week, which had to be some kind of record. I wasn't losing sleep or anything, but bad enough. I should have held it together better for my best friend in front of his boss and all. If he had done that to me at my new job, I would have been pissed.

Then Dexter called the following Friday.

"Dude. You still mad?" I asked.

"Shit, no! Who's mad? I just got hired away by Xerox for twice what I was making."

"How?"

"They heard about the story."

It was all worth it. Life wasn't about being good and playing by the rules. It was about laughing your ass off. Letting jokes fly when they needed to. Those are the times you'd remember. I knew right then I needed to be around friends who "got" me. I was moving to San Francisco ASAP, with or without a job.

# Chapter 32

# San Francisco! Open Your Golden Gates

I set a goal of two hundred dials a day. I had no spare time to ponder the freaks now. I got my rap down to a smooth natural script, instead of saying what I really wanted to say: "Buy something from me, fucker"! Simply put, I was at war. I even started to hang up on *them* if I sensed it was going nowhere. Time was money. Or if they were especially rude, I would call their local Dominos Pizza and send them an anchovy pineapple pizza for them to pay for.

I was numb to rejection and expected it on every call until I got a hold of Nathan Pillsbury. That's the made up name of this guy who ran a huge bond portfolio for a major mutual fund in Boston, which I'll call Shimmerstone Investments.

"This is Nate."

"Jack Fitzpatrick, Freedom Capital Markets."

"Freedom! That's the word of the day!" he screamed. I heard him banging his hands on his desk and giggling, a' la Pee Wee Herman. I looked around the trading floor to see if someone was fucking with me. I even slapped myself to make sure I wasn't in a dream. If this guy was this nuts, surely he would do business with me.

I asked him all the basic questions, but instead of having to pull words out of him like usual, he told me exactly what he was looking for, and even about his business trip tomorrow.

"Know any fun places to go in San Francisco?" he asked.

I did, and I'd be an idiot not to fly up there and be his tour guide.

All the Friday afternoon planes to SF were booked or way too expensive, except for the 747 Pan Am flight en route from Guatemala. Tickets were only forty-nine dollars last minute.

I smashed my carry-on into the overhead, and looked down at my assigned seat. I'd be wedged between a smiling toothless indigenous woman who had apparently skipped the bathing stream before the flight, and a fat, bald businessman whose hot gut oozed over the armrest into my territory.

I was dealing pretty well with these two space invaders until not long after takeoff, when fatty started a stink battle with Guatemala. He leaned over on one cheek with a kind of *take that* look as he released. Mrs. Guatemala smiled even more and bristled in her seat. She was brewing up one of her own.

I was a mature adult with a job now, so instead of banging both their heads together or firing off one of my own in my hand and cupping it under the dick's nose to stop this nonsense, I twisted my overhead air nozzle right at him to deflect the stench. Then I nestled in to try and enjoy the unique sounds and smells of a plane filled with people from a third world country. It wasn't easy, with my affliction of people generally bugging the shit out of me, but we landed without further incident.

Dexter knew how important this night was for me and picked us both up at the airport in his new company car. He told us he was taking us on his "Streets of San Francisco" tour. Dexter's car caught air over selected steep crests, bottoming out the chassis, which made Nate clap like a sheltered six-year-old with cerebral palsy. Between hills, Nate sipped a chilled Heineken from the Playmate cooler that was nestled between us.

Finally, at 3:00 a.m., we were deep in the gallows of Nikki's Bar-B-Q, an after-hours funk bar next to the projects in the lower Haight. I glanced over to Nate, dancing spasmodically with two horny chicks, ecstatic about all the free drinks he supplied. Nate caught my eye and did his awkward clap again, ending with a double thumbs-up. Right then, I knew for sure. He was mine, all mine.

The next week Nate gifted me with a new-issue $4 million Citicorp bond trade with $7,000 commission, as well as something no other client had ever given me: a referral to his buddy who ran a bond fund for another huge firm in Boston. San Francisco could wait a little while.

"Just tell them Nate the great sent you," he said.

I called the man first thing the next morning.

"Hello, Mr. Watson?"

"Who is this? How did you get this number?"

"Nate the great sent me."

"You must be that kid out in California who took him out all night."

"That's me!" What a stupid thing to be proud of.

"I was able to beat Nate at squash for the first time, thanks to you."

"Glad I could help."

"Tell you what. I'm working on a buy program right now. Where can you offer me nine million Ginnie 8's?"

I gasped. Those were as easy as selling Treasuries. I would work for nothing on this trade as part of my plan.

I jerked my eyes up for Phil, but found only Wyatt leaning over crossed arms reading the paper. Shit! Shit! Shit!

"Mr. Watson?"

"Frank. Call me Frank."

"Could I have just a minute? Please?"

"Come on, kid. I'm giving you a bone. I don't have all day. Give me your price." I stood up.

"Wyatt! Offer me nine million Ginnie 8's for good day!"

Wyatt looked around for witnesses, found several looking on in excitement, and was forced to pick up the phone, slowly, plunking out the digits one by one.

"Just a minute, Frank," I said.

"Kid, we're losing the market. I could have been done ten times by now at a real firm." I covered the phone.

"Wyatt, please hurry!"

Wyatt hung up the phone.

"I'm sorry, what did you say?"

"I said, my client needs the price now!"

"I'm working as quickly as I can. Asshole."

Wyatt redialed and leisurely cradled it in his ear until Chanterelle approached.

"Hi, sweetie." She patted his hands like it was his turn for a lap dance.

Wyatt hung up again.

"Beverly!" I yelled. "I've got a trade on the line."

"Sorry, Jack. I just need a couple prices after you."

She stepped to the side.

*Click.* My horse never left the gate. Wyatt smiled as I hung up the dead line.

"Still need those prices, Jack?" Wyatt smirked at me, and then ogled Beverly's breasts.

I threw my pen down and seethed. Then Phil slapped both my shoulders from behind.

"How you doing, pardner?" A toothpick dangled from his lower lip.

"Where the fuck were you?"

"Calm down, boy. Have you seen that hot nineteen-year-old in the cafeteria?"

"Thanks to you, I lost a big one."

"Call him back. Don't be a pussy."

I sat back down and stared at my desk. He knew.

"Well, you still got that one guy. Don't get too greedy."

That was true. I still did have Nate, and if Frank was as important and good as I think he was with his own live trading screens, I probably wouldn't have gotten his pants past his hips.

## Chapter 33

# Don't Shit Where You Sleep

"Jack, we won't be talking anymore," Nate told me the following Wednesday. My heart stopped.

"What'd I do?"

"Relax. They want me to focus more on strategy."

I swallowed hard.

"I hired a nice young lass for you."

At first, I was worried about watching my mouth with Emily, but she was pretty cool, even kind of nasty, and gave me way more business than Nate ever did. I was in the express lane to wave my $3 million in front of Mrs. P until I asked one innocent question.

"What you got going for the weekend?" I expected the same answer she always gave me: hanging out with friends in Beacon Hill drinking mudslides. Then on Monday morning she'd tell me who puked, and I'd say "Wow! You guys are crazy." It was easy.

"I won a free ticket to anywhere America West flies," she said.

"You should check out Vegas," I said. That way she might get laid by a stranger, and it could be our little secret. It might even bring us closer.

"What a great idea! Let's do it! It's only a few hours from you," she said.

What a cruel lesson on how innocent chatter can instantly turn on you. Why hadn't I picked Florida or someplace else that wasn't just down the freeway?

I had no choice but to comply, so I called around Vegas for two hours, everything was sold out, until I found the last two rooms in town.

"I'll take them," I said with relief, cracking my knuckles above my head.

Phil walked up behind me and read my memo.

"Not that shitbox, boy."

"What's wrong with it?"

"You can't take a girl who's looking to get her oil checked to the Union Plaza. She'll get crotch crickets, and it won't even be from you."

"Phil. She's my client." I sure wish he took me more seriously now that I was consistently on the leader board, and rumored to have the next open spot on producer row.

"I'm not kidding. You'll see. That place is so bad they have penny slots."

"But the whole town's sold out."

"Well, shit. I guess you'll just have to look surprised when you check in." He shrugged and patted my head.

Silly Phil. I'm not sure what kind of shenanigans go on in Mississippi, but even *I* knew porking a client could only lead to disaster. But come to think of it, Phil hadn't been wrong yet. Unnecessary phone flirting must be kept to an absolute minimum until after Vegas.

"How will I know you at the airport?" I asked her the day before her flight.

"I'll be wearing red," she purred. I covered my eyes and worried. Just about anything could go wrong, and I'd lose my best client.

I worried the whole drive out there—about Emily, about the Jeep, and about not overheating in the 110 degree heat while keeping up with the solid line of cars traveling 90 mph, inches from each other's bumpers.

At the airport gate, I smoothed my hair in the window reflection. A youngish butter-faced girl in glaring red gauchos walked straight out of the plane toward me.

"Emily?!"

Denying her my love would be easy.

"Do you know where the bathroom is?" she asked, holding her stomach.

"You're not Emily?"

Embarrassed, we both ignored each other at the same moment. Then the first of the flight attendants exited. Could Emily have missed her flight? What a break!

I was just about to click my heels when a stunning marriage-material brunette walked up to me. She wore a red T-shirt and jeans.

"Looking for someone?" she said in a certain know-it-all tone I recognized.

I outstretched my arms, but made sure I wasn't giving her a penis-rubbing Hollywood hug. "It's great to finally meet you face to face."

"I'm relieved you aren't a dog," she said.

Shit! She was beautiful. This was awful. Remembering I booked two rooms at the Union Plaza helped my uneasy forethought of getting drunk and climbing her frame. On the drive to the hotel, I kept repeating to myself, eyes on the road; eyes on the road, but I swear her left nipple was talking to me through her T-shirt.

We made our way through the ash-can-smelling lobby to the front desk. I confidently slid my credit card to an exhausted-looking man in a gray suit who looked exactly like John Waters.

"Congratulations, Mr. and Mrs. Fitzpatrick." The front desk man crept his free hand over the check-in desk to shake mine without looking at me, tapping his cigarette ash with the other. "We have the honeymoon suite all ready for you."

"Sir, we're not married. We have two rooms booked. Here's my confirmation." I pushed the paper over to him.

"We're not too concerned about that here, sir, as long as you pay." The corner of Emily's mouth went up in a sexy grin.

"You've got to fix it," I insisted.

"In fact, it shows here you called four hours ago and changed it."

"Changed what? I didn't call. It wasn't me!"

"Only thing I can offer you now is a roll-out," he said, pointing above his head to a twenty foot banner: "WELCOME ASPHALT PAVERS ASSOCIATION."

"It's fine," Emily shrugged. "I'm okay with it, if you are."

Phil. That fucker! I was going to kill him! I shrugged and let out a nervous laugh while reaching down for our luggage.

"Seriously, Emily. You gotta believe me."

She just nodded.

Outside our door, she ripped the bags from my hands and hopped into my arms.

"Well, what are you waiting for?" she asked.

I hobbled across the threshold with her in my arms and looked around our cherry-scented room, feeling oddly like a Holly Hobbie doll that had turned to porn. Any leftover shred of my Spokane farm-fresh innocence was completely gone now. I put her down on the bed without saying a word and explored the amenities of our scratch-and-sniff museum, fondling the velvet curtains and the like, losing complete track of time. Things seemed to be at a pretty good distance until she found a button that made the bed slowly rotate like the Seattle Space Needle.

"Look at me!" she squealed, seemingly losing 50 IQ points as she stretched out her arms like a snow angel on the flowered bedspread while gazing at herself in the faux antique mirrored ceiling. There was nothing to be gained by pointing out the dried cum stain she was rubbing the back of her hand on.

"All righty then!" I yelled, clapping three times to break her trance. I pulled her up by both arms.

"It's almost ten o'clock, the night's a-wasting!" I wasn't going to bump num nums without a fight, even if she was the hottest thing ever. Vegas or not. I was more than just a piece of ass. I was a businessman, and I had to keep this gravy train running for at least another year or three to solidify my fuck-you money.

Outside, the cement still radiated the heat of the baked-in sun. No wonder this town stayed up all night. It was the only bearable time to be awake.

"Come on, sonny, bring your girlfriend inside. Loosest sluts in town," barked a man who looked fresh out of rehab.

*I've got my own*, I thought.

"Should we go in?" Emily asked, unfazed by his rudeness.

"Free nachos! Just for walking in," the man leered.

Nachos and sluts all in one location. Vegas was dirtier than I ever imagined. I looked above the man's head to remember this joint for Phil. Oh. My bad. What the hell is a "loose slot?"

Emily pointed to the marquee of the Four Queens Casino. "Can we go?"

We ran toward the sign that spelled Frank Sinatra, forgetting the nachos for now, and raced through the revolving glass doors.

"Excuse me," I said, catching my breath to speak to the front desk lady. "Can we get two of your best seats for Frank?"

"There's no tickets, baby," the lady with a silver beehive hairdo answered.

Emily's lower lip puffed out.

"Sorry, Em. We tried."

"Cheer up, kids. It's free. It's Frank Junior, and I bet you can get a front row seat if you hurry." She winked.

"Junior has to be half as good as Senior, right?" I shrugged.

I grabbed Emily, and off we skipped, hand in hand, down the gold carpet like Dorothy and the Scarecrow after a nap in the opium flowers. *Free* was as magic as the word *please,* as far as I was concerned.

"Don't forget, $1.95 New York strips start at midnight," the woman called after us.

Inside the shiny black-floored lounge, we slid into a booth behind a tiny elevated cocktail table and inhaled peanuts, staring at the dim bulbs ringing the stage. Junior finally came on and started crooning like a dog begging to be euthanized.

Bald with large black glasses, he bore no resemblance to his swarthy father. For some reason he chose me, out of his drunken audience of nine, to maintain eye contact with. I must have been the only one paying attention, or maybe he sensed some camaraderie: tonight was leading us both nowhere. I tried to mind meld him.

*Oh, Frank Junior! Riding on your father's coattails is one thing, but scraping along them in the gutter is another. I realize appearing nude in* Playboy, *like your sister Nancy, wasn't an option for you, but what Mafia kingpin made you do this? Stop staring at me.*

"I think he likes you," Emily said, like I'd won something.

I nodded with the beat at Frank to avoid looking at her. But she grabbed me by the knees, spun my stool toward her, and rammed her tongue down my throat, darting it in and out like a Thai woman pummeling green papaya with a stick.

"I like you too." She exhaled hot peanut air on me. My eyebrows jerked up to my hairline.

"I think you're pretty cool too."

I tried to appear calm, pulling an unchewed peanut from her off my tongue, wiping it on my jeans. Now I was doomed. There was no way out. Screw her and lose a client or not screw her and lose a client. I could see Mrs. P doing a cheerleading jump, touching her toes in her brown dress. I hope that dark patch I just saw was underwear.

Pretending this molestation never occurred was impossible while Emily continued to stare at me like Krazy Kat at Ignatz, except I had no brick to hit Emily with to bring her back to her senses. I had only one chance, and it was a long shot. I was going to keep her out all night and tire her out. Then it would be all her fault.

I tried everything. I even threw shots of Tequila over my shoulder while she winced from drinking hers. Nothing worked. The woman stayed perkier and more positive than a suburban Christian youth volunteer during her first day on the job at downtown juvenile hall. Those mudslides from Beacon Hill had cranked up her alcohol tolerance to Jesuit priest level. Even after the 5:00 a.m. group samba lessons at Harrah's, she was still up. We were jogging to the next casino when the strap on her sandal broke and stopped us cold.

"Time for bed." She winked. Shit.

It was time for the big guns. I waited until the elevator doors closed, then pushed my guts out till my face turned red, honking out a loud fart so explosive it felt like I'd ripped something. Emily giggled and tooted out one of her own before she reached out to take my clammy hand.

Back in our room, she modestly put on a pink strappy silk nightgown and brushed her teeth, trying to make eye contact with me in the mirror. The clock was ticking. I barged in front of her and blew my nose one nostril at a time into the sink in a final attempt to kill the mood.

"You're so lucky you can do that," she said.

I was trying my heart out not to like her, but her last comment made her the coolest girl I'd met in years. If and only if she weren't my client, I would have thrown her on the bed and made love till lunch. No, no, no, no, no. Should I? All this pressure. What if I couldn't get hard for her? Should I just eat her out? That was Dexter's trick. He did that when he was too drunk to get it up and thought the girl might report back poorly to her friends about his skills in the sack, setting him back months on the dating circle.

I brushed my teeth until my gums bled and watched Emily teeter out to our round bed. She lay down and turned on the rotator, stretching out like a knife-thrower's assistant strapped to a spinning board.

This was it. It was time. I spit out my mouthful of blood like a prizefighter and charged into the ring to see what would happen. The rhythmic sound of a wild boar overdosing on Valium filled the room. Could it be true? I tiptoed over to the bed.

"Thank you God!" I yelled internally with my arms raised overhead, so as not to wake the beautiful beast drooling spit out of one side of her mouth. I didn't dare turn the rotator off for fear of breaking the spell. Instead I slid into the circle of fear and surrendered. Her hot peanut breath stung my nose hairs in waves. I hoped it might help ward off any unwanted hard-ons.

As one last precautionary measure before nodding off, I built a small fort wall with some of the extra velvet pillows in case of a spooning attack during the fog of the late morning. If Phil was in Vegas right now, he would be dead.

When I awoke around noon with my throat raw from breathing through my mouth, she was gone. Not even a note. My heart sank. The trek home was worse than the drive out.

On Monday, I stormed into the office ready to rip Phil's head off, but his toothy grin disarmed me from sixty feet across the trading floor.

"Was she a quart low?" he asked.

"You ruined the account."

I was too sad to kill him.

"Aw, shit. What twenty-three-year-old wouldn't love what Uncle Phil did?!"

I wanted to tell him everything, so he could see it from my viewpoint, but I just couldn't explain Alain or Hazel to him, and after the "sticker bush incident" with Dexter, I guess I karmically deserved it.

# Chapter 34

# Sugar Momma

I had forgiven Phil after one week, but Emily still wouldn't take my calls. Wyatt eagerly erased my name from the leader board. I was so upset about losing my sugar daddy and his daughter that I laid my head down on my folded arms and drifted off into a depression nap right there at my desk.

I dreamed I was peering down from the rim of a gigantic roiling pot filled with all of Freedom's struggling brokers, all grasping for a leg up, stepping on whoever they needed to just to breathe. We were all in hell, the very bottom of Dante's Inferno. I scooted away on the ledge, but there stood Mrs. Pohlkiss with her arms crossed. I swung around to go the other way, but there was Wyatt. I lost my balance and fell backward into the pot, looking up to see Mrs. Pohlkiss laughing at me, waving her missing black dildo over her head like a pom-pom while Wyatt reached over to goose her.

I woke up and blinked my eyes open toward the producers. If I could just sit near them, I could make money without distraction. I spun my eyes around to the rest of the commoners, dizzied by a confused whirl of gray until I grounded myself on that Irvine wall clock. Who was I kidding? They were never going to let me sit on producers' row. It was officially time to go. I was moving to San Francisco with or without a job—after the Christmas bonus, of course.

# Chapter 35

# Loving Ewe

The mandatory Christmas party was only three weeks away. I'd made it to President's Club this year, entitling me to a worthless plaque, $500 extra on my W-2, and a weekend getaway to a timeshare project in Laughlin, Nevada, that Freedom co-owned.

"Jack, there's an all-you-can-eat buffet, after a short thirty-minute meeting," the owner said, palming his stomach after a loud growl.

"Phil can come too," the owner added.

"That's very kind of you, sir." Phil nodded as the owner walked over to invite the next sucker.

"You gotta get yourself a date, boy. Don't want them thinking you're a fag." Phil winked. "Or you'll never get on producers' row."

None of this shit mattered anymore. Still, it would be nice to have someone with me to witness the fifty freaks and their haggard dates strut down the red carpet in our company's version of the Academy Awards. People would be sporting the latest in tasteless finery, and I would be focused on drinking until my pupils floated.

I really didn't know any girls well enough to subject them to this. There was this UC-Irvine sorority girl, though; she lived next door in a winter rental. Lately, when she was buzzed, she'd come over and give me a blowjob to "practice" for her future husband. I didn't want to invite her because I still wanted her to think I was mysterious and important after I'd left for San Francisco.

There really was only one choice: Cammy, our gum-crackling receptionist. I figured I had a decent chance of getting her to take her gum out for a few minutes to work something else around.

Christmas party night was going to be especially stressful for some of the newest producers, since most hid their successes from their wives.

"You gotta get out now, when she thinks you're poor," Thor told a group of the new trainees. "Then you can get yourself one of these." Thor held up a framed eight-by-ten of his new stripper girlfriend that he'd met through Beverly.

"The more money you make, the nicer they treat you," he said without irony. "Just don't marry them."

# Chapter 36

# Party Time

Phil couldn't qualify for a plaque because he was a trader, so just before the awards, management called him up on stage. Mr. Lincoln awarded Phil a plastic blow-up ewe with a hole in its rectum called a Love Ewe for all his hard work in making them a few million dollars. The former Chanterelle got it at the dildo shop near her old employer Captain Creme's. Clever Chanterelle. The Love Ewe, plus the date she provided for the owner's stoner son, ensured herself at least another month or two on the draw.

"This is not a *Love Ewe*, this is a *fuck you*." Phil grabbed a bottle of tequila from behind the wheeled banquet bar on his way back to his seat and proceeded to fill up the ewe's rectum, sucking out one shot after the other.

"Fuggum," Phil slurred.

I stuck my dinner roll in the ewe's bunger to make Phil cool it, and nodded to the frightened owners that I was doing my part to control him. The real reason was, I hadn't gotten my bonus yet.

The dinner roll put a cork on Phil's temper through the rest of the awards. But then it was dance party time. Phil stumbled over to the owner's nineteen-year-old niece, who was jiggling offbeat in a khaki pantsuit, wearing oversized glasses.

"Would you like to dance?" Phil held out his hand to her.

"No!" She jerked her shoulder away. "Mother!"

"Oh, I'm sorry, you must've misunderstood me. I said you look *fat* in those pants," Phil retorted.

The niece slapped Phil hard on the cheek and ran to the safety of the Lincolns' table. Phil stomped back to our table and grabbed the Love Ewe. He squeezed it with all his might toward the owners, hoping it would pop in a dramatic show of anger. Instead, the dinner roll shot out of its orifice like a potato gun, and embedded itself in the teased hair tower of the owner's wife, who shrieked and batted it out.

"You gotta go, huh?" Cammy calmly chuckled to me around her gum. If she only knew my San Fran plan.

I turned Phil toward the door. He wasn't done yet. He grabbed another dinner roll and hurled it at the dolphin ice sculpture, making it almost topple over. It was a shame he was too mad to laugh.

Phil was so pissed he didn't even bother to show up on Monday. My protector was gone. There was no point in hanging around. I quit on Tuesday, on my terms.

"After all the training and support we invested in you, you're just going to pick up and leave like that? We're family here," the owner said, ransacking my cardboard box to make sure I wasn't stealing anything.

As I stepped toward the side door near the trading desk for the last time, Trusack swooped up, spun me around, and hugged me.

"Good luck." He squeezed my arm. Was this the same line he used on Jeannette?

"I think you're actually going to make it," he said.

It was the nicest thing I'd heard in a year.

# Chapter 37

# CTRL ALT DEL

The next morning, I threw all my clothes in the backseat of the Jeep, just as I'd done in Spokane almost three years ago. I dropped off the plaid couch back behind Safeway for the next kid like me and headed north on Highway 1, arriving in the late afternoon at the Russian Hill pad Dexter had found for us.

It had a view of everything: Alcatraz, the Golden Gate, and, best of all, three twenty-three-year-olds who liked to drink tea, walk around topless and pretend they didn't know we were watching. That was until Dexter ruined it. He came home drunk and stood naked in the window, waving for them to come over. After that, they only did it for me, when they were absolutely sure Dexter was gone.

Before I left Freedom, Cammy slipped me a copy of my trailing twelve months, just over $700,000, as well as contact info for all of Freedom's big accounts. All the biggies—Prudential, Smith Barney, and Solomon—would interview me now, armed with proof like that. I'd just have to leave out that little tidbit about my main client in Boston going bye-bye.

"What makes you think you can make the switch to a reputable firm?" one triple-chinned interviewer at Solomon asked. He was over-schmearing his second company-provided bagel in five minutes. He stuffed it into his hole so indelicately the cream cheese scraped off onto his walrus moustache.

"Didn't I just read last week that you guys got popped for embezzling?" I asked. I was too annoyed to stop my social Tourette's this time.

He pushed his intercom button, his mouth still full.

"Rhonda." He swallowed. "Validate Mr. Fitzpatrick's parking, please."

I didn't want to work there anyway, or at any of these supposed top firms, with their ultraclean mahogany veneered offices with cloud-high views of the bay. They had the same freaks as Freedom, but with even more red tape and a hell of a lot more attitude. I never appreciated being unknown and out of the spotlight when I was living down behind the Orange curtain. Plus, these primary dealers already covered all of my active accounts, including the ones I lied about.

However, there was one New York firm, Green Valley and Co., which recently opened a small branch in San Francisco and was quickly becoming a powerhouse in corporate bonds.

"Sure, come on by. There's just the two of us here," said a sales guy named Johnny. He sounded like he was stoned.

No account conflicts and going from an entire room of freaks to only two sounded very appealing. This would prove to be an unforgettable lesson in quality versus quantity.

I exited the elevator on their floor and headed toward the receptionist. She was a large gray haired woman who was probably fifty but looked seventy. She was dressed in yellow polyester stretch pants and a baby blue T-shirt you might see from Walmart; it had a picture of a cat on it, with the caption, "I'm not fat, I'm just fluffy."

She didn't want to lose her place in her library book, so she kept her head down and pointed me toward the screeching down the hall.

I stopped to lean on the doorway of the room. I was pleased they at least stopped their bickering when they noticed me. This was a good sign.

"I'm Virginia, and this is Johnny," the brunette said, snapping from devil woman into a sweet sorority girl. She gave me a small wave. Her hair was pulled so tight into a bun it gave her a do-it-yourself facelift.

"You must be Jack," Johnny said. They offered me a seat at a desk that faced theirs.

The way she changed her demeanor so quickly was scary, but I sat down anyway, and we talked. I was impressed. They knew a lot more about the markets than I did and weren't afraid to share their knowledge.

"Brah, you should work here." Johnny propped his flip-flopped feet up on the desk and stretched his arms behind his shaggy blond head. "York has no idea what we do." That was his pet name for the home office on Wall Street.

"What time are the morning meetings?" I asked.

"Meetings with who? I don't like talking too much before ten," Johnny said.

"When can I start?"

"Now."

Johnny threw a stack of Green Valley logo stationery at me that proclaimed, "Established in 1880." Of course, if there was anything really good about them, they would have been bought out years ago, but this made me feel good, like conquering South Lake Tahoe. My clients and any others I could scrounge up could remain mine, at least for the near future.

Our campfire ring of desks made it easy to chat in the slow times and to play our daily game of roshambo to see who would buy lunch.

"How come I always lose? You guys are like mind readers," Virginia whined, digging into her wallet. I had no intention of explaining it to her. She always threw down her scissors one beat before our rock, plus her production was twice ours, and she could easily afford it.

"My turn to go get the pooh-poohs today," Johnny said as Virginia slapped a twenty in his hand.

"The what?"

"The killer grinds."

"I'll go with you." I was still afraid to be left alone with Virginia.

Johnny grew up in Hawaii, the youngest of four. When he was twelve, his mother went to answer a phone call in the middle of the night. She tripped and fell, shattering their glass coffee table and puncturing her carotid artery. She died within minutes in front of Johnny and his three younger sisters. It was a wrong number. Johnny's shell-shocked veteran father, incapable of rearing children, farmed them off to different relatives until they were eighteen.

"That's serious, man. I'm sorry."

"Maybe it was good in a way. I learned to fend for myself."

I wish I thought more like he did.

"How'd you and Virginia meet?"

"She was my broker when I ran the portfolio for Far West."

"Are you the one that made it go tits up?" I smiled.

"No, brah. They hired me when it was already a sinking ship." Johnny smiled with a stoned glaze. Even baked, he was the smartest guy I'd met since Phil.

When the Feds finally showed up and locked the doors of Far West Savings and Loan, Virginia offered him a job.

Virginia was the complete opposite of Johnny: a Harvard grad, slathered in the finest makeup money could buy. She wore different cuts of the same dark blue skirt suit. The suits were tailored so tight she could only raise her arms above her head if she took off the coat. And the only time she did that was when she tucked the *Wall Street Journal* under her arm on the way to her morning poo. Neither of us had the nerve to tell her that reading on the toilet was a guy thing, only.

Johnny's relaxed work ethic was a calming balance against the psychotic competitiveness Virginia learned from working in New York.

"How much did you just make on that trade?" She lurched in my face.

"Three thousand dollars," I answered.

Johnny covered his eyes.

"Goddamnit! If you guys weren't talking to me all day! I've gotta take a shit now." Virginia stormed out of the room. She only talked like a trucker when she was amped up.

"Brah, everything goes like candy if she's thinking she makes the most," Johnny said.

"Is that why you leave by eleven to go surfing after you do a trade?"

"Just lop off a zero next time she asks." I'd be ready for Virginia next time.

We soon became the most profitable branch in Green Valley's system, removing any scrutiny on our expense accounts. Not that inventing names of clients for the backs of credit card receipts was that difficult; it just added a certain level of cockiness. Any audit worry about where exactly Mrs. Johnny Rotten worked was gone. My social life went into the stratosphere. Everyone in the bar was my new best friend. I was being used, and I didn't care. Use it or lose it. It wasn't my money anyway.

# Chapter 38

# Paradise Lost

York soon figured out that untrained newbies could benefit from working with us. They didn't have to train them; we did. My stomach knotted thinking of the new parade of unbuffered freaks about to befall us, unmanaged and untrained. I longed for Darwin and Chuckie to keep them in their room until they were ready.

York's first hire was an angry Indian man named Deepak, freshly fired from his last job after he buried a city's portfolio in the same long-term STRIPS I'd sold South Lake Tahoe.

The following week, they hired Noah, a short Jewish guy from Marin whose wife was an inherited millionaire. He thought he had hit the jackpot when he got married, happy to just laze around and coordinate the nanny. But his wife soon demanded he find a job, any job, as long as he was out of the house for at least ten hours a day. His variety of freak was the just-get-the-fuck-out-of-the-house-you-drive-me-nuts group like football-titted Marilyn at Freedom, except his kids didn't visit him in the office during meal times to suck on his tits. With Noah's new job, his wife could now live the life she always wanted, being able to show off to the neighbors that she was normal and had a real husband with a job and everything, at least while Noah was away. Life is about compromise. Nobody gets everything they want.

Before Green Valley, I imagined Noah at a neighborhood barbecue in Marin. "What do you do for a living?" someone might ask.

"Nothing, just living off the wife. She's kind of a bitch, but it's worth it!" he would say, adjusting the cufflinks he took from his dead father-in-law.

Now he really was different. He got to say, "bond broker." That sounded cool and powerful, even if in reality he made nothing. If Green Valley stopped his draw it didn't matter a shit bit of difference to him or York. Brokerage offices were set up to run like theaters. Our branch was already profitable, so any sales from the Jujubes and Hot Tamales (or in our case Noah or Deepak) were gravy. The only way to get fired now was to bring a gun to work—and maybe not even then.

York's hiring of people over the phone was even more lax than Freedom's. So I was shocked when the hottest chestnut-haired twenty-four-year-old ever strolled in a week later. Laila. Oh sweet Laila. She was a gift to the earth. It was momentous. You never know when you are going to meet your future wife. She was sassy and smart, and way overqualified for her position of answering phones and journaling our trades. I was happy she was around, just so I could look at her. Although good things always come to an end, it usually takes longer than two weeks.

"Goddamnit, woman! You will do as I say, or I will cut your clit off!" Deepak yelled at Laila for leaving off a few preposterous fake receipts on his latest expense report. His outburst left me confused at whether to laugh at the absurd thing he said or cry because I knew she'd walk out.

"Do it yourself." She tossed the report in front of him.

"No woman will talk back to me!"

I stood up to defend her.

"Do not interfere with my people! She works for me!" Deepak scolded me.

This tripped me up just enough to where all I could do was watch her storm off toward the elevator, never to be seen again. I was devastated.

Virginia smiled, an odd smile, like she'd shat her pants and was squishing around in it, happy there was someone in our midst just as crazy as her. Now any male attention would be back on her.

Our mandatory busywork of journaling trades piled up without Laila. We were desperate for a special person that could handle all this dysfunction: someone between a young girl who didn't want to work too hard and an old mule who could handle our rudeness. That's when tattoo-covered Darlene strolled in the door for an interview. She was way too cool to be a freak. Even I could be schooled.

After her first few weeks, we began to look forward to the old hippie stories she'd share.

"Be sure to wear flowers in your hair," she recalled. She made sure she had them as part of her outfit when she hitchhiked out to Haight Ashbury in 1967. She came all the way from Phoenix after her mother refused to believe that her stepfather had molested her. She was fourteen.

Other stories about having a three-way with the porn stars from *Behind the Green Door*, getting addicted to heroin, and sleeping inside Goodwill donation boxes for shelter seemed like a scary movie to me.

"How'd you finally go legit?" I asked.

"This trick I met on the Sausalito ferry who worked at Merrill."

"You hooked on the ferry?"

"Rush hour was the best time for business."

"How'd you feel about being a whore?" Virginia asked, making me wince.

"How do you like being one?" Darlene fired back, smoothing her long brown hair behind her ears.

Virginia had nothing to say. It was awesome.

Darlene made our lives better. She was a soothing Mother Nature who buffered the back-and-forth bitching with New York. She worked so well that New York had to find a new way to fuck with us.

"We're cutting your payout 5 percent on desk trades," they said one afternoon. Just because. New York didn't know how to act when there wasn't any conflict. We squawked plenty, but it was useless. Upper management was a bunch of smiley old guys who got their cut for doing nothing either way.

"You kids just work it out," they said. And since the New York asshole traders were right in their faces every day, they won.

So *we* worked it out. We fixed it so they would get nothing. Green Valley's value-add to its clients was a faxed inventory of hundreds of corporate bonds with their current market value. Bonds they really didn't own, but made markets in, just like the other big dealers.

If a customer called in to buy a bond on that fax, instead of calling the trading desk like we were supposed to, we frantically searched Lehman, Merrill, Smith Barney, or anybody's inventory to see who offered it cheaper.

We couldn't call the dealers directly, so we used our favorite hedge fund customers to buy the bonds directly for us. They often negotiated an even better price, and kept a small cut for the hassle. That way, the trade would appear as a "cross" instead of a dealer/customer trade, and we got to keep all the commission. York knew exactly what we were doing but could never prove it. We were unfuckable with. For now.

# Chapter 39

# Trailer Parks R Us

Things were so rosy at work that Darlene invited me over for dinner at her place in the mostly black city of Richmond, north of San Francisco. Dexter and I had not been out of San Francisco much, so I invited him to join me.

We followed Darlene's directions, which led us past a burning trash can surrounded by black men warming their hands over the fire and laughing. I'll admit, I was a little scared.

We continued straight ahead into a trailer park abutting the northernmost depot for the BART train system.

"Dude, this is like a private island of white-trash," Dexter said.

We were just about to give up and head back when we saw Darlene, happy as hell, waving at us, standing next to the orange flames of a freshly lit Hibachi in front of her white single-wide.

"Don't say a word," I insisted to Dexter before rolling down the window.

"Hey there! I didn't think you'd show up if I told you about where I live," Darlene said to our widened eyes.

Boy, did I feel like a sheltered prick. I mean, I grew up poor—or at least I thought so—but I had never even been in a trailer park, let alone a trailer, at least one without an engine built into it. Who needed a trailer in Spokane when a house like Mom's cost $35,000?

Darlene invited us inside. We walked up her makeshift cinder block steps.

"See this stove?" Darlene pointed to a light green porcelain miniature gas range. "It's a Dixie. Worth more than the whole trailer."

I pumped my legs up and down, like I had in the elevator with Wyatt.

"What the hell are you doing?" Darlene steadied herself on her pink sparkle Formica countertop when I got her trailer rocking.

"Just want to give the neighbors something to talk about," I said with a grin.

Darlene opened up a side window. "Give it to me!" she said, before whooping out a rebel yell to one-up me. She shook her head and smiled.

"Those days are over for me, and they all know it."

That night we smoked pot, barbecued ribs in her asphalt yard, ate seconds of homemade mac 'n' cheese, and got introduced to damn near the entire trailer park. Funny thing was, I got along better with them than most people I'd ever worked with. Where was the trailer trash I'd heard so much about? Maybe there were a few too many guys in wife beater tank tops, and a few too many with missing teeth, but that was it. They were real people, with real hopes and real dreams, straight from the heart.

"Why don't you leave here?" I asked.

"It's only $500 a month for the cement."

A bone-chilling SCREEEECH blocked out the next part of her justification.

"That's a lot of money for the privilege of hearing Bart trains all night."

"Don't forget about this excitement." Darlene pointed to the ceiling where she'd patched a few stray bullet holes with JB Weld.

"We've gotta get you out of here."

"I own these four walls outright. Who wants a payment?"

"You do."

"For what?"

"For a write-off on your taxes."

Darlene was silenced for the first time since she started working.

Within three days, Dexter and I found her a two-bedroom condo for $99,000 on a busy street in Walnut Creek for no money down. Her

VA loan after taxes was only $500 a month, and there wasn't a guy wearing a wife beater on the whole block.

"Baby. I don't know how I can repay you." Darlene squeezed me tight.

"Yeah, I guess giving me a blowjob in the stairwell would be kind of weird, wouldn't it," I said.

"That's it!" Darlene spanked me.

"I was kidding." I said.

"You'd last five seconds with me," she said, shaking her head with her finger to her mouth.

"Then what are you thinking?"

"I'm going to be your broker."

She meant our happy hour broker, finding girls for us each night at different bars, with free drinks supplied by the unlimited company credit card.

"Just make sure they have a little dirt in them, Darlene."

"Don't we all. Don't we all." She shook her head.

"Like I told you, I'm not looking to sign up Mrs. Fitzpatrick until I'm at least thirty-two."

Darlene just smiled and pointed skyward. "That part's not up to you, Jack."

## Chapter 40

# Bar Brokering

Night after night for over a month, Darlene whispered a few sweet nothings into the ear of our agreed-upon girl. Within minutes, I was grabbing my coat to bang out my animalistic desires in my attempt to find the deeper meaning in life.

"What are you telling them?"

"A girl can't reveal all her secrets." Darlene patted my shoulder while sipping her trademark gin and tonic through a thin black straw.

Never, ever underestimate how efficiently a third party can chat you up, saving you hours of small talk to close the deal. It was the power of the wingman, times two. There was some sense behind those arranged marriages.

Two weeks later, what I really wanted was for her brokering to slow down a little. My winky was getting kind of chapped, and I was getting a bruise on that bone beneath my pubes. But I am not a selfish person. Darlene was having so much fun helping me out, I just couldn't let her down.

The next night we found ourselves at Pier 23 Bar, washing down top shelf margaritas, in between wolfing down plates of fried calamari that could have used an extra three minutes in the grease.

It was now about an hour after sundown, and the fog had just rolled in, stealing every bit of heat from the day. I had just returned from assessing my beaten-up equipment in the bathroom.

"You better take this with you tonight." Darlene reached into her Macy's bag to hand me a box that might house a dozen roses.

Inside was a black dildo the size of an eight-year-old's arm, even bigger than Mrs. P's model that I threw off the cliff at Liberty Park.

"Jesus!" I used my entire body to block it from view, just as a curly blonde cutie headed toward the bathroom and winked at me.

"Is that her?"

"I might have said too much this time." Darlene shrugged.

"Too much! This is inhuman. And it's black! Is it new?" I sniffed it.

"Of course it is. I just bought it." She blushed without too much embarrassment.

"Is this what you've been telling them?"

"This one was a tough sell. I had to sweeten the deal a little bit."

"Good lord!"

"Be sure and clean it before you give it back," she said, putting the cover back on the box.

"Why did you buy this?

"Well, you know. Dating has been kind of slow, what with working all the time and the new condo."

"You weren't really going to use this, were you, Darlene?"

The bathroom door slammed open. The music and voices seemed to go silent as the curly blonde sauntered up like a Western outlaw with Spaghetti Western music in the background. She rubbed my stomach.

"You ready to release that monster?"

"I guess so."

Darlene patted me on the back as I stood up. She raised a clenched fist at me for confidence.

"Need a ride?" I asked the blonde.

"All night long," she purred. "You're coming back to my place."

As soon as we got through the door of her Polk Street studio, the fun was over. She threw me down on her bed and ripped my shirt open.

"Slap me," the girl said. I did.

"No, dammit, with *that*." She eyed the box and rubbed her cheek. I took it out, and on the first swing of the bat I smacked her too hard again. She jumped up to examine a growing pink welt on her temple.

"Way to go, asshole. My customers are going to think I got hit by a big dildo or something."

"Tell them a picture frame fell on you." I said, since she was the assistant manager for Fast Frame on Van Ness.

"Just leave."

Although I was supposedly in charge, once again, I left feeling used and dirty. It was just like the night with Hazel, but I was the one to blame for this situation. I headed for the door with Darlene's box under my arm.

"Should I call you?" I turned and asked out of obligation. The girl grabbed her "friends and family coupon" she'd given me for 25 percent off from under my thumb pressed against the box before she slammed the door on me.

Where were all the nice girls? Or did everyone just want the same thing? I needed to take a breather from Darlene's help and just be me.

Back at my apartment, I pulled up a chair to join Dexter on the veranda. He was sipping a Heineken. His feet propped up on the ten-story-high railing.

"I just don't get it." I said.

"Well, if you ask me, I think girls want to figure out you're a good guy *after* you fucked their lights out, not before. Then you buy them the burger and fries and do all the courting stuff."

"Why's that?"

"Because if you suck in bed, they'll be really mad they didn't get at least a steak out of you."

I didn't understand what he said either. Why was life so complex?

## Chapter 41

# Work My Fingers to the Bone

The next day I stayed late to help Darlene sift through the day's tickets.

"How'd you know I had a big dick?"

"I didn't," Darlene said, not even bothering to look at me.

"What if I didn't?"

"It worked, didn't it?" she said, smacking the tickets on her desk like a deck of cards. "You're never going to see them again anyway."

"How do you know?"

"They're sluts to you."

"Is that what you think?"

I had never felt so empty. Hooking up just for the hell of it was always so great. But now, it suddenly wasn't. The need for sex was right up there with food and water, I thought. What else was there?

"Darlene. What's wrong with me?"

*Plenty*, she said with her eyes.

"I mean how come these girls aren't doing it for me?"

"Have you ever tried dating anyone that wasn't white?"

"That's it!" I slapped my thighs and raised my hands to the sky. "Hallelujah!"

That was my problem. It was so simple. That's why I left Spokane. At least I think it was. I needed diversity, and now I lived in a place where I could easily do something about it. I wasn't following my dream.

It was time to venture out on my own to sample the world. I had never dated an Asian girl, or a black girl, or a Filipina, or any girl that wouldn't get seared to a crisp after a couple hours at the pool. I'd heard that once you go black you never go back. So if that was really true, maybe I should try contracting yellow fever first. Conveniently, I lived just a block away from Chinatown.

There was a cute Asian girl I'd been eyeing in my office building for a while. She went to lunch the same time I did, but she would never meet my gaze. I started by letting her walk into the elevator first, pushing back the black rubber seal so the door wouldn't close on her. Cheap, but solid gentleman stuff.

"What's your name?" I finally asked, the daddy of all pick-up lines.

"Ling." She kept her eyes on the ground. I could tell she thought I was cheesy.

"Like Bing?" Shit. It was obvious she'd never heard of Bing Crosby.

"No, like Cha-ching," an Australian guy behind her chimed in, pulling his arm down like a slot machine, saving me from excavating my way to China.

Ling spun around and socked him in the chest. There was something very refined about the way she hit him.

"Naw, she's a good girl. Give her a roll," he said just as the door opened so he could avoid her next fist.

"He's worse than my brother," she pouted.

"I was just going to lunch. Want to join me for some Chinese food?"

"Chinese food? Too greasy. And the meat. Who knows what it is? Why do white people always ask me that?"

Her accent made her more intriguing.

"There has to be one place you like," I pressed.

"Well, there's Sam's. My uncle owns it."

"Wanna go?"

She shrugged. I took that as a yes and stalked her up the steep part of California Street toward Grant. We waited for the light to change at the crosswalk opposite the McDonald's with Chinese lettering.

As we stepped off the curb, a vehicle flashed in front of our faces. It was a white minivan driven by an Asian man. He sped through the red light, nearly killing us all.

"Fucking Asian drivers!" a fellow near-victim muttered beside us.

"If I hear one more white person complain about Asian drivers, I'm going to scream!" Ling scowled at the man in a suit, giving me just the right opportunity to put my arm around her to protect her. "You white guys are always honking at us, making us nervous," she said to me.

I nodded. Those assholes.

It was just then, for the first time, that I noticed that most Asians really do suck as drivers, even the guy waiting in his Camry at the stop sign at the next crosswalk. He looked straight ahead, instead of in all directions. It was clever in a way, I suppose. This way we had to look out for him, and he could do whatever the hell he wanted. But that kind of behavior deserved the occasional honk and societal shout-out.

Now before you call me a racist white boy, I know this isn't the only group that pulls this. I had witnessed it before in Spokane with soccer moms in screaming-kid-filled station wagons, or with little old ladies driving like Mr. Magoo. But this was different.

Here in Chinatown they brought the no-eye-contact trick to the street so you'd have to skip out of the way. That's something you could never pull in Spokane, where a Mrs. Pohlkiss type would yell, "rude," or a cowboy might block your way on the sidewalk for the fun of it, until you acknowledged him.

Over our next few dates, I saw no point in bringing up my revelations to Ling and setting her off, especially because we just did a lot of hand holding and closed-mouth kisses. But that was about to change: Ling was taking me to her Sunday family dinner.

"You'll be the only round-eye." Ling smiled as we strolled in to her auntie's living room, which was filled with the chatter of eight women. Their words sounded like bullets ricocheting off metal. If that wasn't stressful enough, the dining table was set with chopsticks only. Sure, I had used them before, to stab food, but in front of this audience I might have to go hungry if I wanted to make a good impression.

I sat with my hands folded at the black lacquered dinner table and watched matching black bowls with red insides being filled with steaming rice. How many years of practice did it take for them to master the art of elegantly picking up a single grain of rice? My hand cramped up just thinking about it.

I watched the far side of the table where the gynarchy of her great-aunts sat. They had to be master chop-stickers. Each looked like Margaret Thatcher gone Geisha with their black-dyed Aqua-netted hair.

It was time. In unison, the aunts began. I took a breath and mimicked the elegant way they picked up their sticks, slowly moving their cradled bowls an inch from their lips. Then, and only then, did they start shoveling it in! I scanned the rest of the table for looks of horror, but everyone else was doing it too! I felt so tricked. It was an insider secret they purposely failed to share with the rest of the world.

I wasn't going to waste any more time being good. I flicked the whole bowl in my face in five moves, just like them, and smiled with my mouth full at the auntie who had a mole with a two-inch hair growing out of it. Auntie glanced over at Ling and moved one of her chopsticks in and out of her mouth. Was she implying Ling would give me a blowjob later? That dirty auntie. I thought I was imagining things until I looked over at Ling. Her face was beet red, and she was muttering something in Chinese, scratching her nose with her middle finger at her aunt.

"Jack grew up in the mountains, Auntie."

"Oh, with the beaws?"

"Bears," Ling whisper-translated to me.

"He had to kill one once, didn't you, Jack?"

Ling kicked me hard under the table, forcing a nod out of me.

"Oh. You live on like the Ponda-rosa."

"Yes, ma'am," I responded. My performance tonight ensured I was getting laid later, plain and simple. Ling knew it.

This family dinner made me jealous of Ling in her role as the rebel. What if I brought Ling home to shock Mrs. Pohlkiss?

After the chilled canned lychees, the aunties soon tired of speaking English with me, and started blinking a lot, adding a yawn or two and dabbing their eyes. It was a polite cue for us to leave.

"Mountain boy, you come back soon," Aunt Hairy Mole said, patting my butt. She winked at Ling.

We walked back through Chinatown toward Ling's apartment, peering in all the overly lit trinket shop windows, until we stopped at the blanket of a homeless guy selling his wares.

"Take this," the scraggly bearded man said, handing me a used "Beginner's Guide to Kama Sutra" manual.

"How much?"

"Just take it," he said. I threw him a five-dollar bill.

Back at her place, with our new book, we had no choice but to make love for hours, not missing a position. We got our money's worth.

I considered myself more open-minded than the average bear, but I wasn't quite sure how putting our ankles behind our heads was going to get us off any better than the regular way. However, it was a great excuse to have sex, and gave us both something to strive for.

"Will you be faithful to me when I go to Shanghai?" Ling asked, with our noses pressed together in an especially sweaty athletic position.

Ling was leaving in six days for a month-long visit with her relatives.

"Yeah, sure," I said. Faithfully having a good time. What was she talking about? I expected her to go wild in China.

There was no need for drama. We would either hook up when she got back, or not. If fate popped something sweet in my lap in the meantime, I wasn't going to say no.

That next week, Ling and I didn't really speak until I took her to the airport. Even then, we still didn't have much to say, so I fiddled with the radio until the dial stopped on that J. Geils song, "Centerfold." Just as I was about to bust out in full karaoke, another Asian guy in a white minivan shot across four lanes of traffic on the 101, forcing me into evasive action onto the shoulder. I swear it was the same guy from Chinatown.

"My blood runs cold! My memories have just been sold. Der-der-der-der-da-duh, look out for the Asian in a minivan." I sang, calmly swerving back on the road.

Ling's eyes widened like I'd called her mother a whore.

"What did you say?"

"You like this song too?" I asked. She knew I could get out of this one. The words fit perfectly.

I dropped Ling off at China Air and felt a strange sense of relief as a 747 deafened me overhead. I felt like I was the one taking flight, free from Ling's angry disposition.

On my way back to the city, I exited at Bayshore Boulevard and pulled into one of those fifteen-minute oil change garages. Those places always took much longer than that, so rather than stress out and be forced to read bad magazines in a smoky two-seater waiting room, I walked over to the Old Clam House, established in 1864, taking it on faith that it wasn't a strip club filled with old ladies.

Inside the rough dark bar were cauliflower-faced regulars hashing over San Francisco stories from forty years ago. But at the far end of the bar, a lesbian couple looked as out of place as me. One was a hot, perfect-bodied redhead, while the "man" looked like she could kick my ass. Her hair was buzzed military tight around her ears and left long on top and in the back. Not a good look by any stretch of the imagination, but I guess this way, guys wouldn't even consider hitting on her.

"Nice hair," I said, like I meant it.

"Short on the sides for Dad, and long in the back for the daughter Mom never had," she said, making me laugh. The redhead gazed into my eyes.

"I'm Jack." I reached out my hand to Red. The butch one shoved her hand out first and shook mine.

"Lazer, with a Z."

"And you are?" I asked Red.

"Jackie."

Lazer didn't like Jackie looking at me. She grabbed Jackie by her chin and gave her a long kiss. Not a bad move. I was going to have to incorporate that into my own game sometime.

I bought the next round of drinks, and the next, and moved my bar stool closer, one round at a time, until finally I was right next to Big Red.

"Hey, pussy. Let's arm wrestle," Lazer said.

"Okay, whoever wins gets to kiss Jackie."

"That's what you think." Lazer put her elbow on the table, ready to go.

Lazer had no idea I was dorm champion, but experience told me to lose this match after a realistic struggle. It was like letting a kid win at checkers so their confidence could glow for a while, before you sent them to bed with a pat on the head.

"Fuck, yeah!" Lazer yelled, slamming my hand down onto the sticky bar. Jackie fell right into my scheme and doted over my red wrist.

"Can you kiss it?" I pushed out my lower lip at Jackie, unable to resist winking at Lazer. That started us man-to-man on a tequila shooting contest, which led to the kissing contest. Jackie was the sole judge, and we carried on until somehow we ended up at Jackie's apartment somewhere in Bernal Heights. I was now apparently over the trauma from Arthur's sex party.

As soon as the door closed, the girls dropped to the couch and started making out without a word. I kicked off my shoes, tore off my shirt, and stepped out of my pants. It was a perfect day not to be wearing underwear.

I couldn't believe my amazing luck. I patiently hovered over them for the perfect moment to wedge in on the fun. By this time I was sporting a huge woodie and decided the most polite way to join in on the party was to tap Jackie on the head with my throbbing proboscis, otherwise known as a friendly cock-slap.

Bad idea. Lazer looked up at my unit with a mixture of rage and jealousy and growled. Jackie's eyes were fixated on my wand like it was glowing.

"Put 'em up."

Lazer hopped up from the couch and put up her dukes, circling me like a boxer, her exposed bowling pin shaped breasts screaming out for a bra. My hard-on should have faded instantly, but it didn't. So I started to laugh. Lazer took her chance and in a blur threw me out, naked, and slammed the door in my face. The door opened a second later. My clothes.

I sat down on the cement walkway overlooking the parking lot and put on my jeans, not even bothering to brush off the tiny bits of gravel embedded in my cheeks. It was official. Threesomes were out for me on my round-the-world tour. There would always be an odd man, woman, or she-man out, and I wouldn't want to put someone through the kind of rejection I was feeling. I was a one-woman guy, if I could just find the right flavor.

# Chapter 42

# The Beginning of the End

Work had been smooth for many months. Everyone, including New York, was making enough money to leave each other alone. But then the head of the "cage" in New York, the place where they clear trade tickets, was found dead of an apparent heart attack. He was only thirty-seven. Death happens all the time; that part isn't crazy. But when the death occurred just after the auditors discovered $15 million missing, then we have the makings of a movie of the week. The next day, the FBI arrested Green Valley's in-house auditor and compliance officer.

It wasn't like these back office guys stole it from Green Valley, or even a customer's account. These were criminals with a conscience. Crooks who stole from Eleanor Rigbys: inactive accounts that had no heirs.

When people die, unclaimed accounts are supposed to go to the state, but these back office employees, pissed at the millions that traders and salesmen were making, decided it was their turn. They funneled all the dividends and interest generated by these dead accounts into a fictitious account to which only they had access.

For the first time, the bosses weren't smiling. The NASD slapped us with a $10 million fine and forced our holding company to fire all the smiley guys.

I didn't give a shit. The story made page four of the *Wall Street Journal*. It wasn't my company. I had no room for this in my mind. And only one of my customers—who hardly did business anyway—read the

*Wall Street Journal.* The dead guy was conveniently cremated within three days before they could do any autopsy, but they did determine the ashes were from a dog.

Later that afternoon on my walk home through Chinatown, I needed to clear my head, so I fixed my eyes low to secure a straight path. There, waiting on the corner of Kearny and Pacific, was the most squeezable butt ever, swaggering right in front of me, just begging for the full-on Charmin treatment. It was as if two Nerf cantaloupes were fastened beneath the small of this young lady's back.

I followed the orbs until she stopped at the next corner. Those pants had to be custom made. There was no other way the melons could fit. Then a chocolate-colored palm waved in front of my eyes. I followed it up to a beautiful brown face. She smiled.

"Hi." She offered her hand. "You haven't seen a butt before?"

I actually blushed.

"Not like yours. Not where I'm from." Girls loved it when I sounded like a hick, because it made me sound harmless.

"Where you from?"

"Spokane."

"Isn't that up near Canada or something?"

I would tell her about my sophisticated Russian Hill address later.

"Where they do all that Aryan Nation stuff?" she added.

I hated she knew about that. Guess I'd have to work the farm boy angle more and show her a little Spokane hospitality. Then she might oblige me with a feel of her beautiful butt.

"What's your name?"

"Shaniqua," she said, like a slow soul song.

Even though we just met minutes before, we walked along the crowded street and held hands. It was nice, natural, and not forced. I watched people's eyes for some kind of shock, some judgment, because she was black, but there was none.

"Can I see you tonight?" I asked.

"That'd be nice." Nice and natural.

By the time I got back to my office, I was beaming. I really *could* live my life just the way I wanted.

"Baby, a Wyatt is on the phone for you. He's called three times," Darlene shouted. Of course, it had to be Phil playing a joke, because that dickhead trader from Freedom would never call me.

"What do you want, you fucking prick!" I said, holding the headset to my ear.

"I suppose I deserve that, Jack."

It was him! It was really Wyatt!

"I'd like to apologize," he said.

All those nights I sat up dreaming of beating the shit out of him, and then he wanted to take it all away from me with a sorry? Fuck that. I stayed silent.

"I heard you're doing really well up there, and I was wondering if you'd like to do business."

"Pardon me?"

"Offer me ten million long bonds."

"Are you serious?" Old buddy, ol' pal.

Turns out he owned a money management firm that specialized in trading the thirty-year bond. This was a coveted type of account, because all you had to do was state a price off the screen and execute the trade instead of wasting time searching for a specific bond.

"It's 104-21," I said, padding an extra 1/32 into it for myself. He was getting off cheap for all the pain he caused.

"Done. Thanks."

That was $6,000 to me. I had no anger left. Seemed like my anger was worth a lot more than that, but it wasn't. What a validation: a former enemy calling me to put trades in my lap.

# Chapter 43

# Easy Street

"Honey, you sound so good." It was Mom calling me on Saturday morning.

I *was* doing well. Plus, I had spent plenty of time imagining the shock and joy of bringing Shaniqua back to meet Mrs. Pohlkiss. Shaniqua wielded much more power than Ling, a mere Asian.

"Mom, I've met someone."

"That's terrific. What's her name?"

"Shaniqua."

"What a pretty name. Where's she from?"

Uh, *Africa*? I wanted to blurt, but I stayed silent and got strangely scared. Of course, Shaniqua was a black girl's name. Such a fun name, I found myself repeating it over and over during my afternoon walks home. I said it high and low, fast then slow, as I walked. Even the homeless on Broadway didn't panhandle me now.

Would Mom approve? Would I care? Mom had barely been out of Spokane.

"She's from here, Mom."

In the end, I knew the color of her skin wouldn't make any difference to her if I loved Shaniqua, but I didn't want Mom to worry. Mostly, I didn't want anything to bring me down from my double high.

"Did I tell you the Langdon place was for sale?" she asked.

That was the beautiful stone mansion across the street from the Pohlkiss place, with an even better view.

"No kidding? How much?"

It was so cheap. I couldn't believe it—$450,000 for almost ten thousand square feet of what had to be the nicest home in Spokane, built by one of the owners of the Northern Pacific Railroad. I sometimes did their lawn when the gardener was on vacation, and would peek through the windows to admire the dark box-beamed ceilings and built-in mahogany cabinetry.

And so it was decided. I had saved just enough to buy it for cash. It was going to be a surprise for Mom. My dream of showing up Mrs. Pohlkiss was all coming together.

I didn't even have to fly up there. I just called up the listing agent and wired the money. They even threw in some of the furniture because I didn't negotiate on the price. Spokane was a small enough town where word traveled fast. I wanted everyone to know I was a baller. Mom was finally going to be better than Mrs. Pohlkiss. It was the best feeling of my life.

"Mom! Guess what!" I told her the next week.

She knew better than to ask, "What?"

"You're moving to the Langdon place, Mom."

Longer silence. I expected her to jump up and scream, maybe even cry tears of joy. The landmark she'd admired her entire life was now hers, sort of.

"Are you there?" I asked.

"Well, honey. Wow. How? You're joking, right? That sounds like a lot of work. You didn't really buy it yet, did you?" She kept babbling on and on, stunned.

If she wasn't going for it, it's not like I could just take the place back to the store and say I changed my mind. The deal was done, and Spokane real estate moved slower than sitting through Sunday morning service with a hangover.

"I'll hire maids and gardeners."

"You should keep your money for yourself, honey."

That's when I started to get mad. Didn't she realize this was going to change her life? Maybe a guy of Dad's caliber would finally see her worth and sweep her off her feet.

"Jack, aren't you even going to come up and see it? You haven't been home in three years."

"Christmas, Mom. I promise."

By then I would have another half million in the bank, and I could shower her with presents, and furnish the place the way she wanted.

"Mom, think about it! Now you can hang out with Mrs. Pohlkiss."

"Just what I've always wanted."

I was the only one allowed to be sarcastic; she knew that. Mom couldn't dampen my spirit this time.

The dream of Christmas caroling across the street at Mrs. Pohlkiss's house with my new black girlfriend was making me giddy. But fantasies about my new great relationship were better than reality. Shaniqua didn't get a lot of my nasty jokes, or ever seem to like them, even when I spelled them out for her. I was also getting annoyed that every time I suggested meeting her parents, she'd change the subject. Ling took me to her family dinner on our fifth date. Shaniqua and I were way past that now. I was angry and felt cheated from my daydreams of a backyard barbecue with funk music and huge purple shiny '70s cars that bounced up and down.

It was time to speed up the process. Tonight I was going to show her I was down with her culture by taking her to Henry's BBQ on Divisadero before Soul Implosion night at The Box.

After twenty minutes of looking for parking, we found a spot on busy Fell Street and walked the four blocks to Henry's. It was especially cold and foggy, even for someone from Spokane.

The front windows of Henry's were opaque, caked with years of grease and steam.

"I'll take care of us." I motioned Shaniqua to a booth in the back and then stepped to the counter to order a full rack of ribs with all the sides. I walked back toward Shaniqua with my green plastic tray piled high. She was waiting for me in a red sparkle vinyl booth, busily flicking leftover corn kernels off the table one by one. What was I doing wrong? Maybe she was just hungry.

I plopped down our lattice baskets and started right in, covering my face with sauce before looking up to notice she'd barely eaten a corner off her rib.

"What's wrong?"

"It just so, so …"

"So what?"

"So Fred Flintstony and messy."

"I thought you guys loved these." As soon as it left my mouth, I knew I was fucked. Where was the rewind button?

"*You guys*? I grew up in Palo Alto."

I could only stare.

"Not East Palo Alto," she added matter-of-factly. "My dad's a professor, and my mom's a psychologist," she finished, not as much mad as disappointed.

I wiped my sticky face and stared some more.

"I think I better go." She reached out to shake my sauce-basted hand.

"Can I drive you home?"

"No. Thanks. I can take the bus."

"No. Really I want to."

"It's fine. They're letting us sit up front and everything these days."

I deserved that. I finished wiping my face with a towelette and watched the bus swallow up Shaniqua and roar away.

# Chapter 44

# Becoming Celibate

I was officially giving up dating. Priests had it easy. Nobody was right for me, and I didn't know how to fix myself. How could I make myself fall in love, make myself blind, just for the sake of being with someone? It was now painfully clear that society was scared shitless of young single men running wild, screwing their daughters at will—or maybe even their wives, if they stopped by the Red Onion on certain nights. Society wanted you to settle down. Be normal. That must be the key to happiness, being normal. Then everyone would finally stay off your shit, and you could relax. I'd just have to get rid of my Jeep, buy a K-car, get some khakis, and blend right in.

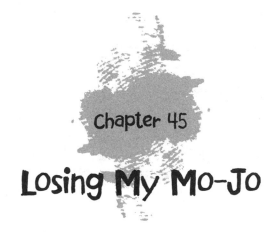

# Chapter 45

# Losing My Mo-Jo

The only thing good in my life right now was business, and that was boring. I could do no wrong. I didn't even have to make outgoing calls any more. Sure, I was grateful for making butt loads of money, but I was starting to wonder what the point was. I had no one to share it with. There are only so many cocktails and steaks you can gorge yourself on before you just get fat, get a red face, and never stop yourself. You already look like shit, and there's no turning back.

Even this last good thing in my life, the money, was beginning to get harped on by Virginia, who figured out the real size of the trades I was doing.

"You know, that Wyatt guy is just day trading," Virginia whined, pointing to the Telerate screen where my trade just printed. "Where is he safekeeping bonds? Does Silverman know about him? Nobody would just do trades with *you* like that."

"Why not?" I asked.

"Because you're not me! I am the player!" Virginia slammed her fist down on her desk. There was no calming her down this time. Something else was wrong. Virginia flipped open her compact to look in the mirror.

"Fuck," she said, patting her puffy eyes. "I haven't slept in two days."

And then she got a phone call.

"Yes. This is Mrs. Winston. What dinner reservation for two?" she screamed.

"My husband is on a business trip!" Virginia slapped her palm down on her desk. "No, keep it. Keep it; that's fine. I'll be there." Virginia hung up and lion-roared at the ceiling. "I'm gonna catch that sonuvabitch red-handed."

Johnny and I considered going and sitting in a nearby booth, but even we were way too afraid.

The next day Virginia showed up reeking of alcohol. Her third day with no sleep.

"That fucking bastard has got another thing coming if he thinks he's going to get any of my money. Half of nothing is nothing."

Her husband, a Harvard business grad himself, didn't feel the need to work right now, with his wife pulling down so much money. He had plenty of time and her paychecks to go out and be bad.

"He can work on his 'spiritual being' without me!"

Virginia ran out of the office and returned an hour later, panting at the doorway.

"Jack, get off your ass and help me." Virginia dropped five overloaded plastic bags filled with one liter value-sized bottles of Jean Nate body tonic. She shook her fingers to soothe the deep, angry red lines from the heavy bags. Walgreens was a difficult place to spend your life savings so your ex husband would get nothing, but I admired Virginia for giving it a shot. Even insane, she still looked for value.

"Guess who I saw downstairs in the lobby?" Virginia shoved her left eye close to mine like a nearsighted Captain Bligh.

"Who?" I covered my nose to block her distillery breath.

"I said, guess!"

I wished it was a man in a white suit to take her away, but instead I offered, "A clown?"

That would be on par with her current state. I hoped she really did see one, and it would make her feel normal.

"A clown?! No, you fucking idiot." This no sleep thing made her sound like she'd grown a set of sweaty balls. "Laila."

"Laila who?"

"You know. Fucking hot bitch that used to work here. The one whose clit Deepak wanted to cut off?"

"Really?"

"Yeah. I gave her a bottle of this stuff on the street." She untwisted the white bottle cap to inhale it like a breath of fresh air. "She loves me now and wants to come discuss things."

"Like working here again?"

"She's a fucking lawyer now, dumbass. I'm gonna fry that fucking husband of mine's ass."

Laila appeared at the door holding her own two-year supply of Jean Nate. She looked more beautiful than ever, calmly leaning on the door with a smile just for me.

Was I number one in her beat-off memory bank, like she'd been in mine since the day she stormed off? I bounded over to her in two steps and kissed her without saying a word—long, deep, and passionate. It was an out-of-body experience.

"Jack! If you think you're gonna take credit for my Jean Nate, you better just fuck off. You dicks think you can just control a girl with a kiss." Virginia jumped up and ran over to our newest sales assistant, Bart. He was fresh out of college and still a league rugby player. He had no problem ignoring Virginia's outbursts while leaning over his *Sports Illustrated*. Bart was the complete opposite of me with his outward desire to please everyone at his new job. He was a big teddy bear. The kind of guy who could be sweet because he was so huge. He could squash anyone like a bug if he wanted to.

Bart looked up at Virginia, hovering over him. His eyes widened to a low grade of fear. Then she flung her leg over him and straddled him, ramming her tongue down his throat and bouncing up and down on him like a Hippity Hop.

"See, Jack. You're not the only one who's got it." Virginia grabbed Bart's hand and pulled him up. "Come with me, Bart, we're going shopping." Bart looked over at me for help, but all I could do was shrug, selfishly happy she was now occupied.

He would get a great employee review from me, if we had those kind of things.

Laila and I stayed in the office and talked like old war buddies until the nighttime cleaning crew drowned us out with their vacuums. There were no thoughts about keeping the conversation going. We could just *be*. This was a first. I was finally in love, and I knew it.

Virginia showed up the next day at work more whacked than ever. She had stayed up all night doing cocaine with Bart to celebrate the fact that she'd bought his-and-hers baby blue Porsche Carreras, for cash, at the dealership.

"Bart, you know you can't keep that." I leaned down toward him at his desk.

"Tell her, not me," he said, holding his throbbing head.

"It's done, sweetie!" Virginia yelled over to Bart. She had booked two first-class tickets around the world, and they were leaving tonight on the redeye.

"I can't go. I've got rugby practice," Bart complained.

"You bastard! You're going!" She screamed and cried, pounding on his solid chest with a tirade of nonsensical sayings while Bart did his best to hold her swinging fists.

"I'm going to kill myself!" Virginia ran down the hallway and hopped in a waiting elevator.

Bart and I reached the parking garage just in time to watch her squeal away in her new Porsche. It didn't even have plates on it yet.

We had enough sense not to chase her, and instead called the police and gave them a full description. The police found Virginia an hour later parked at the end of the Sausalito Pier sitting on the slanted hood.

"I'm filming a commercial," she said to the police as she was handcuffed. It became clear why society locks up their crazies. It's not to protect them. It's because they sure are a hell of a lot of work for everyone else.

With Virginia now locked up for eight weeks in Ross Psychiatric Hospital, an eerie calm took over the office—a quiet that made me feel like prey being watched. Like something really bad was about to happen.

It came in the form of a phone call, the way everything always did at our work. It was from our new currently corruption-free back office.

"Jack. Your customer Wyatt didn't pay for his ten million Treasuries."

Crazy Virginia wasn't so crazy after all. One day of interest on a failed delivery was equal to my commission, and more. I panicked, about to stain my underwear, when Wyatt called back.

"Sorry, kid, I forgot to enter the trade."

I didn't know if he was lying or what, but the customer was always right, and I didn't want to ask too many questions. I liked the trades. Mostly, I didn't want anything to ruin my lunch today with Laila.

Close to noon, I glanced over at Deepak. He seemed to have stopped breathing. His face blushed, and his eyes darted down to his desk in shame.

Laila must be here. There she stood, twinkling her fingers, clitoris intact and all, letting Deepak know there were no hard feelings. Laila owned Deepak now because he said something so rude to her, and she forgave him. She was such a cool and beautiful being. She owned me, because she *was* that cool and beautiful being.

# Chapter 46

# Love American Style

Walking down the street with someone I loved was a wonderful feeling—that pride, that sense of wanting to show the world I had something great. It was a feeling I hadn't felt since Montana used to pull me around on my skateboard.

Before Mrs. P hired me to do her lawn, when Dad was around, I used to take piano lessons, twice a week. I was pretty good too. I could play "Claire de Lune" with no sheet music. Stuff like that. But we didn't have a piano, so I had to practice before my lesson in the basement of the music store next to Color Tile on Division. After Dad died, I wanted to quit, but Mom guilt-tripped me big time. She'd say stuff like, "Your father is watching you quit," and other choice Catholic guilt lines like that.

So when Dad died, Mom got all nicey-nice with Mrs. P, which of course was weird because Mom never liked her in the first place. Now they had a lot in common, with the dead husbands and all. Mrs. P got all charitable with Mom and offered her the job of being her maid, suggesting I come over to practice after school and play with Charles. After Mom finished her work, we got to go home to our servant's quarters across town in Hillyard. Piano was okay, but with a deal like that, I was more than willing to let the piano lessons and Charles go.

Mom finally wore me down so I'd make it a regular thing. Mostly, I was getting a little lonely going home to an empty house. I agreed to go every day, but only if I could bring Montana.

"I suppose that would be okay," Mrs. P said, knowing I wouldn't come without him. "Charles, he can be your dog, too," she added.

And so it went. I practiced piano for about an hour, or as long as I could stand to watch Charles play with Montana. It still bugs me to this day to think about it. Charles touching the dog my dad got me was like watching some guy scratch behind the ears of my girlfriend and pat her ass.

Montana was loyal to me and didn't like Charles much. I knew this because Montana refused to go outside with him while I practiced, so Charles stayed inside.

I told Charles at least a hundred times: don't touch Montana's butt while he's sleeping and don't mess with his food when he's eating. Two simple things I told him, over and over. Montana was a pound dog, and must have had a hard life before we found each other.

About two months into this bad arrangement, Mom was at Rosauers doing their shopping, and Charles was especially anxious to go outside. Montana was sleeping, probably faking it so he wouldn't have to deal with Charles. I was three minutes into "Swinging on a Star." I was no lounge act. I couldn't talk while I played or I'd lose my place in the song. There are parts in that piece so difficult that you have to spread your fingers wider than a dinner plate to make it sound right.

"Are you done yet, Jack?" Charles asked me like he always did, but it was especially annoying that day.

Usually I'd let him ask a few more times and ignore him. Then, when *I* was ready to quit, I'd act like I was giving in and tell him to make some sandwiches for us. I timed it all out perfectly. How I wish I had stopped early that day.

Charles touched Montana's butt. Montana had finally had enough of his teasing. Montana lunged up and bit Charles in the face, right on his lip. By the yelps from both of them, I knew it was bad, and jumped over to Montana, who was cowering, very sorry he had lost his temper.

Stupid-ass Charles. He knew! He was supposed to be so smart. Mrs. P came running down the stairs.

"My baby, my baby. His perfect face." She pulled Charles's hand away from the giant bite on his lip. "You did this, Jack." Over and over she said it, while I held Montana by his collar.

Mrs. P ran to the kitchen and came back with a Ziploc full of ice. I felt so bad that I even held the bag on Charles's lip while Mrs. P called Doc Driscoll.

"I'm not putting that filthy dog into my car," she yelled into the phone, but the Doc said Montana needed to be tested for rabies. I should have never let Montana go without me. We should have run down the street and escaped. But I was weak. I could just imagine how mad Mom would be at me for disobeying Mrs. Pohlkiss, plus I didn't want to get her fired.

I realized now, walking down the street with Laila, that all this time I've been mad at Montana for biting Charles. Just mad, though; I didn't want to kill him. I watched Montana drive off in Mrs. P's big blue diesel Mercedes. I never saw him again.

"I'm sorry, Jack. The doctor said once he's tasted blood, he'll want more," Mrs. Pohlkiss justified.

My ears rang. Just like the time Mom told me Dad died. Montana wasn't a wild animal. That was a lie. No way was I ever going to go to their house again, ever.

Mrs. P never really apologized, but she did offer to buy me another dog, even two dogs, but nothing was going to bring Montana back. Then she made me an offer I couldn't refuse. If I did her lawn, she would pay me $500 a month, an absolute fortune for a twelve-year-old.

I sold out. When I first went back, I ignored Charles for an entire month. I just watched him kick his shoe into the lawn while I worked.

"I'll give you my authentic remote controlled Speed Racer car. And my new ten-speed! Just look at me, Jack!" He called out.

I knew how much he loved that car. The day he gave it to me, I invited him out to the corner of his yard, put a little gas on it from the lawn mower and burned it right there in front of him. He seemed glad, thinking we were even now, but we weren't. Not by a long shot. (If you're wondering, I kept the bike.)

It's funny what things make you think about other things. I probably would never have gone out to make all that money if it weren't for Mrs. P. I know that now. Being with Laila was chipping away at my anger without even trying. She made me want to quit my job and just hang out with her. I didn't have anything to prove to her.

I also tried fighting getting fully attached to Laila, but all my resistance was being sucked into the wind like the white fuzzies of a dandelion. In the end, Laila was just plain better than Montana. (Sorry, Montana.) She could talk, but not too much, like most girls. And she only talked about cool stuff. I think that's what I liked most about her. Oh, and the sex, of course, which is awesome, but I'm not going to talk about it because she'd get super pissed.

Today for lunch, I was taking Laila up to Chinatown, away from all the white folks in suits. Anybody can spend money, but only the clever can find the perfect combination of price and tastiness—like at Ling's uncle's place.

At Sam's, I could feed us both for about six bucks, provided we ordered the water served in thick red plastic cups instead of splurging on a grease-cutting Coke.

This sunny Friday was too perfect to eat inside and pretend Sam's moving wallpaper wasn't teeming with cockroaches, so we headed down to the cement wall at Portsmouth Square with our Styrofoam containers to watch the old Chinese guys playing checkers.

"Fifty cent extra for to go," the waitress said, trying to get some kind of tip off me.

Outside on the street, I reached into the thin pink bag for an egg roll and blew on it so Laila could have the first bite.

"Hawt," Laila breathed outward, fanning her mouth and gazing at me with her hazel green eyes.

It was impossible not to kiss her, even with her mouth full of greasy cabbage, slow and passionately as if the world stopped for a moment to let the egg rolls cool down. Then a voice screeched behind me.

"You only like me for sex time; see if Asian girls are tight." It was Ling, appearing out of nowhere like the Wicked Witch of the Far East.

"Why you no call?" Ling insisted, poking my shoulder.

"Why *you* no call?" I replied.

"You know he'll cheat on you," Ling screamed at Laila.

"And you! You feed her the egg rolls from Sam's, just like me. He my uncle. No your uncle. You no come here."

I held an eggroll up to Ling.

"Want one?"

She slapped the eggroll from my hand, splattering the entire container on the ground.

"So you like big American pussy better? Huh? I bet you can hear echo on her."

To be totally honest, I couldn't tell the difference.

Ling lurched toward Laila with her fists clenched. Laila stood staring in silent shock.

I stepped forward to protect my girl, and grabbed both of Ling's hands just in case she decided to use them. There was a smush as my foot zipped out from under me and accidentally accelerated my hand onto Ling's face. Hard. Really hard.

Ling doubled over and held her eye.

"Shit, I'm sorry, Ling." I bent down to comfort her, one foot in the gutter and one foot on the sidewalk.

"It was an acci—" *Wham.* I was flat on my stomach in the street in handcuffs. I peered up to a young Asian policeman who looked even angrier than Ling.

"I saw everything," the officer said, shoving my face into the mashed egg roll with his boot. "Are you okay, Miss?"

Ling shook her head and muttered something to him in Chinese.

"Do you want to press charges?" he asked. Ling nodded.

"It was the egg roll," I protested.

"An egg roll did this?" The officer pointed to Ling's eye. "Assault and battery is a serious crime."

"What? Tell him, Ling. I would never hit a girl!" I yelled.

Ling fixed her eyes to the ground, shyly, before darting a nasty glimmer at me with her remaining good eye, letting me know that this was only the beginning.

"Do you need a doctor?" The cop leaned over to Ling, who nodded like a lost little girl. Ling made a face at me, stopping shy of pointing her finger at me. The officer radioed for an ambulance.

"Ow!" I yelled as the officer jerked me up from the pavement by my cuffed hands and stuffed me in the patrol car.

"Don't hurt him," Laila yelled, her expression a jumble of concern, anger, and disbelief. "Why are you doing this to him? You know it was an accident!" Laila pleaded with the cop.

"Move away from the vehicle, or you are going with him."

Laila had no choice but to watch me drive away.

# Chapter 47

# Hard Time

If you haven't been arrested, let me be the first to tell you, it really sucks. First, they take your wallet, watch, and anything else you have, and put it in a manila envelope.

"Take off those weapons," the check-in officer commanded.

"What weapons?"

"Your boots! Now!"

This had to happen the one day I wore pink ankle socks. Pink because Dexter threw his stinky red workout shirt in with my laundry. It was going to be impossible to look intimidating now.

Then I was off for fingerprints and mug shots, just like in the movies.

"No smiling, or we're just going to stand here," the warden insisted. Geez. It was just instinct.

"Next to child molesters, woman bashers rank a close second," the deputy barked for all to hear. "Looks like you get to stay here all weekend," he beamed.

"What do you mean?"

"First available court hearing is Monday morning."

*Fuck.*

The same deputy led me into my cell. There were no iron bars to run my tin cup along, just four walls, no windows, and a pay phone for collect calls. What a disappointment.

Dexter would be home early from work and on his second beer by now, feet up on the balcony railing, priming himself for the weekend, just like I was supposed to be doing.

"This is a call from a San Francisco County Jail inmate," the recording said once the phone connected. You couldn't talk over it—further humiliation to remind everyone you'd been bad. It also kept horny inmates from prank calling unsuspecting housewives.

"Dexter?"

"You gotta be kidding me, Jack?" It was so good to hear his voice. Finally someone to lean on.

"Help me, dude."

"Did you get cornholed yet?"

"Man, this is serious. I hit a girl."

"Was it one of Darlene's tricks?" I was never telling him about my exploits again.

I stared into the phone, baffled at his lameness until the cell door opened. A giant six-feet-five black man sauntered straight up to me and stood with his crotch at eye level.

"Off the phone, bitch. Max gots to make some calls."

"I'm busy," I twittered like Sean the model. Shit. I covered the phone to mask Dexter's cackling and made my eyes into mean slits. Real mean.

"Squeal like a pig, boy!" Dexter roared. I couldn't wait for his turn in the slammer. I was surprised it hadn't happened yet.

"You're gonna be busy later unless you get off, *now*." The giant black ox smiled and patted his huge bulge.

"I gotta go, dude."

"Some chick named Alice called. She sounded old."

I hung up.

"All yours," I said.

"Mine's bigger," the black man said, grabbing the phone from me and twiddling it between his fingers.

I didn't dare look back. I crawled up on my bunk, pulled my sweater over my head, and pretended I wasn't here; instead, I was hiding in a childhood fort made of sheets.

"Fitzpatrick, you've got a visitor," the guard said. I popped my head out like a turtle.

"Who is it?"

"Do I look like your fucking secretary?" The guard walked over to my bunk and knocked me to my feet with his billy club. He pushed me into the hallway. Max didn't get treated this way.

"Sir, do you think it would be possible to get my own room? I mean—"

"Shut it."

"What about innocent until proven guilty?"

"You've got ten minutes."

I searched the pea-green room for the Plexiglas wall and the two-way phones, but it was just a room. I walked over to the window. It overlooked the 101 freeway just before the Bay Bridge. I wished I could hitchhike out of here and forget the whole thing.

"Who are you looking for?" A familiar female voice snuck up in my ear.

It was the brightest spot of the week. It was Alice, not looking a day over thirty-six, smiling and shaking her head. I hugged her until her boobs turned into pancakes.

"That's enough." The guard rolled up on the balls of his feet, reveling in his power trip.

"How'd you know I was here?"

"That stoner roommate of yours."

"Dexter?"

"I knew he would never give you the message, so I called back."

"It's so great to see you." I touched her hand. The guard glared. I pulled back, not wanting to lose a second of these ten minutes. I needed every ounce of her attention to fill up my love cup. Alice grabbed my hand back and smiled at the guard, unafraid.

"Alice, I hit a girl."

"Not my little Jack." She hugged me again. "So let me guess. You broke up with her. She fainted and banged her head on a curb, and now she wants you to pay for the stitches."

"It was an accident." I strained a smile for her.

Alice got behind me and started in on one of her trademark back rubs. Goose bumps.

"Thanks, Alice."

"Sounds like you haven't talked to them yet, have you?"

"Talked to who?" I asked.

Alice stopped her magic fingers and sat down.

"The Feds."

"What?"

Alice leaned forward and kissed my forehead.

"You really don't know, do you?"

"Just tell me."

"You've been selling bonds to Wyatt, haven't you?"

My stomach sank. Those kind of Feds.

"Shit. What happened?"

"I warned you to stay away from Wyatt."

"What happened!?"

"The unemployment number was the complete opposite of what everyone thought."

The room grew dimmer.

"He doesn't have any real customers, does he?"

Alice shook her head. The number one rule in our business was to know your client. I knew my client, and he was the slimiest asshole I'd ever known. Of course Wyatt was trading for his own account all this time. I should have known. How could I have been so stupid! I guess I did know, deep down. But just like a fat girl in a miniskirt, I pretended everything was just fine. I was even taking it one step further and sporting a terry cloth tube top.

I wasn't the only one Wyatt screwed over. He needed a posse of us willing to look the other way. A herd of greedy, lazy brokers who worked at shitty firms like mine, sick of kissing ass for business. All he needed was one broker to buy the long bond from, and one to sell it to when the market moved. That's the only way it would all work.

"Remember that big insurance company in Iowa?" Alice asked.

"Yeah. You made 150 grand in one trade."

"Wyatt got me that account."

"You didn't do anything wrong, did you?"

"Hell no. Baby, if I was doing that, I would have made a lot more than 150K. But if I stayed, Freedom would take their half, I'd have to cut a check to Wyatt for half, and then pay the portfolio manager for the rest. Screw that."

I jerked forward. "Why didn't I think of this?"

"Time's up, Fitzpatrick," the guard said, sauntering his crotch inches from my shoulder. Guys in prison sure like to put their dicks in your face when they talk to you.

Alice stood up.

"Wyatt told them you did it. That it was your idea."

I buried my face in my hands. The guard jerked me up by my collar.

"And another thing, sweetie," Alice added. "If someone asks if you want to be a caboose in their train, tell them you don't want to play."

"Thanks. I appreciate that." People should be a little more compassionate about their jokes when you're in prison.

"Oh, come on now," she said. "Chugga chugga, choo-choo!" She pulled her arm down on an imaginary air horn. "Cheer up."

The guard walked me back down the hallway.

"We moved your cell," the guard said.

"Thank you. That huge guy would have killed me."

In my new cell on the top bunk lay the same monster guy, rhythmically kicking the heel of his tennis shoe against the cement block wall like water dripping on a rock. I'd seen enough TV to know to act tough early on, so I puffed out my chest, stood on my tip-toes, and waited for him to turn around. He never did. So I crawled in the lower bunk and punched my pillow in between his beats.

"You sure are a tough little white boy." He peered down.

"Thanks. Where you from?" I asked.

"Marin."

"Really?"

"Don't look so surprised. Marin City actually. It's the only place they got for us black folks in Marin." Max laughed.

We started talking. Max was buds with Tu-Pac Shakur at Tamalpais High. He even sang a few of his own originals to prove it, inspiring me to sing mine about the Asians in a minivan.

"Man, that ain't no rap song. There's no soul, no sex. That's more Weird Al Yankovich."

I guess it wasn't the right time to tell him I liked rap music about as much as country. And if you think about it, they are the same thing: one whining about the high cost of a forty-ounce, and the other twanging about a trailer door not closing right.

"Try it again. This time sing about some pussy that got away or something."

Max wouldn't take no for an answer.

"Click, click goes my candy stick," I rapped.

"If I was you, I wouldn't be singing about hard-ons in prison, especially with that little butt of yours." He had a good point.

Our singing grew louder as the night wore on. We were drunk on life—until the rest of the cell block freaked out on us, and the guards demanded we stop. They probably just wanted to be included, but the front stage was only so big.

We continued our ditties in a whisper, busting tear-filled laughter into our pillows whenever we hit upon a perfect verse.

I hadn't had this much fun since freshman year with Dexter. I was starting to like it in here. The world outside was filled with people who wanted to take me down. But inside, I had no worries, and the scariest guy in here was my protector.

Max and I slept till lunch on Sunday and strolled into the cafeteria fashionably late. It was clear everyone wanted to have us at their table. We were the kings of the wing, sitting alone in the corner facing the room. I was just waiting for somebody to look at me cross-eyed. Then Max could smack his fist into his hand, forcing the enemy's eyes to the ground, just to show he could. I was his bitch, but I didn't care. He was mine too.

I tried calling Laila almost every hour to tell her about my new friend and not to worry, but after the prerecorded prison message, all I could hear was crying. Then she hung up. Every time.

"Hello, Mom?" Yeah right! I would have sooner died than made that call. What if she told Mrs. P? Information like this would keep her living to be 110.

I hoped Mom was happy living in her new mansion. I just wish I hadn't bought her such an expensive one; now all my cash was tied up. Never put all your eggs in one basket. That was the number one rule of investing. I just didn't think my basket would get knocked over so soon.

At least the guards were much nicer to me now. Since I arrived, Max had become a model prisoner. He shouldn't have been in here either, though.

"You got a good public defender?" one guard asked me after he stopped by to join us in a rousing version of "Swing Low," complete with hand motions.

"I made too much money last year," I said.

"You're fucked then," he said.

"If you treat someone like a criminal, they'll act like a criminal. If you treat a girl like a bitch, she'll act like a bitch; and if you give anyone power, they'll take it," Max philosophized.

"Amen, brother." We high-fived.

I was happy to let the State of California take care of me. I had paid my taxes for almost three years. They owed me. They could have all the power they wanted.

But I kept thinking I must be repenting for something. This whole jail thing must be some kind of karmic bitch-slap. I recapped everything I had done wrong in my life. Things I knew were bad. Like stealing Mrs. Pohlkiss's favorite joy stick, or selling South Lake Tahoe long bonds, or telling Dexter's boss I was going to throw her in sticker bushes, or hitting Ling, or splitting the profits with the portfolio manager. Hold on! Not the last two.

# Chapter 48

# Kangaroo Court

Courtrooms are set up for a true walk of shame. I sat on the left side with Max and another convict who was in for armed robbery. All of us were dressed in orange neon so everyone could identify us. I still wore my pink anklet socks. All the DUIs and stuff like that sat on the right side. They didn't have to wear orange.

Hard-timers got called first to get us off stage. In return for prompt service, we provided entertainment, similar to the way people slow down to view a wreck on the freeway. Everyone was glad it wasn't them. I kept my eyes to the ground, in case someone recognized me from the happy hours around town.

"Mr. Fitzpatrick, do you have a lawyer?" The judge addressed me through his microphone.

"No, sir."

"Why not? Shows here you made $420,000 last year. That's not chump change."

The audience gasped. They'd crucify me. Society loves to bring you down if you've left the herd.

"It's all spent, sir."

The judge shook his head.

"Appoint him a public defender," he said to the bailiff. "Can you post the $100,000 bail?"

"No, sir."

"You don't need to come up with all of it, just a small percentage. How about $10,000?"

I shook my head.

"$5,000?"

I kept shaking.

"I'm not going any lower; $5,000 bail." The judge banged his gavel and mumbled something to the prosecutor.

"Earliest hearing is Thursday."

I shrugged and looked over at Max. He was my bro. My homey. I wasn't going through this alone. He had my back. I tried to remember I was having fun. Wait, who was I kidding? This fucking sucked! Get me out!

Max was up next.

"Can I stay?" I asked.

"Move it," the guard said, shoving me out of the room.

I tried to amuse myself on the walk back, thinking that I might finally come up with a rap song Max would approve of. Maybe Max would have some more true stories from the hood for me.

It was my turn for the top bunk tonight, the position of honor. I climbed up and rolled on my side, covering my exposed ear with my bicep, and drifted off into a sleep that wasn't sleep. I could hear everything around me, except I couldn't move. My life raced in review, stopping at key parts. I saw Alice and her C-cups, Ira chasing me in his wheelchair, and Darwin holding the Chuckie doll in front of my face.

"Go ahead, pull 'em down. You know you want to."

Then everyone from Freedom, even Mrs. Pohlkiss, stood above me in my prison bunk bed while I lay naked under the sheets, nestling with Chuckie while he smoked a cigarette. He grinned like he'd taken advantage of me. They clapped, all of them, louder and louder. It was the applause I never got for my first trade.

Wyatt's face spoke in slow motion.

"You're the reason I need a drink. I'm going to do everything in my power to make you fail." Mrs. P pumped her fist in the air like the Chess King had at the mall.

I jumped from my prison bed and flew through the air to karate chop Wyatt, but he couldn't feel it. He just laughed. I shouted at him and slapped him with both sides of my hand, but he wasn't moving.

"You fat fuck," I screamed, but he still wasn't flinching. He wasn't changing. I couldn't change anybody. *I couldn't change anybody!* I could only accept them as they were, greasy comb-overs, pigtails, and all.

I woke up to Max laughing.

"What's Nu-fa-fuk?"

"What time is it?"

"Time for this nigga to be going home!"

"You're not leaving me here, man." I sat up.

"The hell I can't, sly." Max patted my head like a dog. "Ain't no one gonna mess witcha. I already got T-Bone and Jay-Fli working the program for ya."

The guard came to the door.

"Jack. FBI is here."

FBI sounded serious, worse than the Feds. It sounded like "going away for a long time" if everyone got their way.

"Don't go anywhere till I get back." I pointed at Max.

"Crackuh, the second that gate opens, I'm outta here like a greyhound."

I walked past the other cells and felt the stares. The cozy home club I'd created with Max was gone. T-Fli and Jay Bone didn't give a shit about me. I was fresh meat.

Inside the stark interrogation room, two dark suits waited under the florescent light with a pocket tape recorder and two yellow legal pads.

"All we want is the facts," the blond one said in a deep voice. His face was sunburned everywhere except around his eyes.

"Am I under arrest?"

They both looked at each other.

"Yes, you are."

"I mean by you guys."

They looked at each other again.

"Not yet."

"Cool. You forgot your sunscreen."

He patted his forehead.

"Look," I said, "I've really never done anything wrong, except for selling long bonds to South Lake Tahoe, smoking pot, and occasionally drinking and driving when I couldn't find a cab."

The blond one fumbled with his tape recorder.

"What was that again?" He held the recorder near my mouth.

"I said I've done nothing wrong."

He snatched it back.

"You've got the wrong guy," I demanded.

"Wrong guy for what?"

"Wrong guy for whatever it is you think I did."

"What is it you think you did?"

"Whatever it is that you think I did, I didn't do it."

The red faced man slammed down his hands on the table, volleying an echo off the walls. His partner looked away to hide his smile.

"This is about Wyatt, isn't it?"

"So you know." They looked at each other and nodded and then started nodding to me.

"I know that fat prick is a lying shit, is what I know. I used to work with him."

Red face grabbed the recorder and pushed rewind.

"We don't need your opinion, just the facts. Tell us about Centurion Insurance in Iowa."

"That wasn't my account."

"Whose was it?"

No way was I turning in Alice.

"I don't know."

"You do know!" he said, slamming his hand down again.

"And what about Shimmerstone Investment?"

"Look, if Wyatt did something wrong, nail him, not me."

"We will, Buster. We are not a bunch of morons. We can make your life very difficult."

"You buds with T-Bone?" I asked.

"We're going to put down in your file that you were uncooperative."

"Fine. You can't hurt me. Can I go now?"

Max was going to love my story, sassing back and all. I was always such an ass kisser whenever I got in trouble. This felt good.

When I returned to my cell, a scrawled note lay on my bunk pillow. CALL IF YOU NEED ME NIGGUH, I'M LISTED.

I should have been happy for him, but I felt sick. How could a complete stranger become the best friend I'd made since Dexter?

But I wondered if society would make it tough for Max and me to hang out. My new city friends would probably see him as a novelty, an amusement, or Max would think they were too tight-assed and wouldn't want to get to know them. Then somebody would offer to let him paint their house, thinking they were doing him a favor, and everything would go sideways, and I'd have to choose sides. Dammit. But for now, I had a black friend! It was something I had always wanted since that movie *Brian's Song*.

Going to lunch without Max was going to suck. My soul was empty. I couldn't open up, and the chance of finding another Max was zero. Plus, lunch today was meatloaf.

The cafeteria stunk of rotting flesh, from more than just the entree. I grabbed a banana and coffee and sat in the corner as far away from everyone as I could get, including T-Bone and Jay-Fli, or whatever their stupid nicknames were. They ringed a table with three other tough jamokes, all talking with their mouths full, holding their forks in their fists.

"Hey, pussy-boy. You ain't got no protector no more, do you?" taunted the largest of the tattooed white boys. Jay-Fli, the one who Max said would protect me, just looked down at his powdered mashed potatoes. Shit.

"You think you're better than us?" asked the one whose face looked like it had been smashed by a shovel.

He was asking one of those rhetorical questions I learned about in college, the kind you're really not supposed to answer. It's not that I thought I was better; we just didn't have anything in common. Okay, maybe I did think I was better. Better because I didn't lick my fingers after every bite, better because I flossed my teeth sometimes. Better because I was innocent! I could go on.

"What do I look like, Mother Teresa?" I answered in my best Brooklyn accent, not realizing they would have no fucking idea who she was.

"What you say about my momma?"

Tattoo guy rose and charged at me. I held my lunch tray over my head, but he punched through it like it was Styrofoam and connected square on my eye. It stung like hell. I snapped into survival mode, choosing to live, and in a millisecond was up on the chair performing the same flying karate kick from my dream. My cheap prison-issue tennis shoe struck Tattoo's jaw and sent him to the ground. There would be no survivors.

"Fight! Fight! Fight! Fight!" The roar of the cafeteria fueled me.

I scanned the room, numb with adrenaline, ready for the next person to step into the ring, but seconds later I found myself face down in handcuffs, again.

"We don't need the preppy kid kicking the mean guy's ass," the guard said.

"Why the fuck not?" I asked.

"The whole system would break down if that happened." The guard jerked me to my feet.

My right eye was swollen shut by the time I was back in my cell. The guards insisted I take my meals alone in my cell until my hearing.

My hearing took a first-grader's year to arrive. I was going to post bail no matter what. Sell the Jeep, the remnants of my soul, whatever it took. My days of martyrdom were over. The judge was right: I was John of Arc, except now I was pulling myself off the stake, walking off the pyre, ready to swing against anyone telling lies.

I tended to my wine-colored eye at the sink and wetted my fluffy blond hair, which stuck straight up, doing my best to look less like a crazy person.

"Fitzpatrick, it's time." The guard gently walked me to my seat in the courtroom. I was still afraid to look into the crowd.

"The State vs. John Henry Fitzpatrick," the bailiff said.

"How are you today, Mr. Fitzpatrick?" the judge asked.

My nervous public defender pursed his lips at my appearance.

"Dandy," I said, looking the judge straight in the eyes with my remaining good one. My defender moaned.

A pair of eyes from the crowd burned a hole in the back of my head. I turned around. Ling. Damn. Sporting her own formidable shiner. She pushed her way through the waist-high swinging door, dressed in a steel gray polyester pantsuit. I was terrified.

"Your honor, if I may," Ling said with no accent. She cleared her throat to continue. I hummed "God Bless America" as loud as I could. The guard stood with his crotch in front of me to stop, so I did.

"I would like to drop all charges," Ling said matter-of-factly.

The DA looked up. The judge shrugged.

"Mr. Fitzpatrick, you are free to go."

My heart jumped! I wanted to lift my handcuffs over Ling's head to hug her, but I'd probably break her ribs from excitement. I just smiled instead. A fake smile, but it was a smile.

The blond FBI agent swooped up to the microphone.

"Your honor. Christopher Williams, FBI." He shouldered me out of the way.

"Your honor, we believe Mr. Fitzpatrick is a flight risk. We have serious charges and evidence against him in a separate matter."

"And what might those charges be?"

"Embezzlement, securities fraud, interstate trafficking, and tax evasion."

"Bullshit, your honor," I yelled.

The judge waggled his finger at me like the pendulum of a metronome.

"What proof do you have?" I asked.

Behind the agent appeared that awful prick Wyatt. His hair had grown long into a Dutch Boy cut that made him look like a bloated Benjamin Franklin after two days face-down in the river. The FBI agent put his arm around Wyatt, but there was no hiding the fact he was still the bully on the playground, the one nobody wanted to play with, but did so anyway so they wouldn't get beat up.

"Wyatt is the head trader of a major brokerage firm in Southern California."

"Major! With one employee," I blurted.

"We have evidence that Mr. Fitzpatrick inflated the commission of his trades and then split them with certain portfolio managers, defrauding innocent investors of their rightful gains."

"That's a lie! I've never even thought of something like that."

"What's your evidence, Mr. Williams?" the judge asked.

Williams produced a cardboard apple box filled with client statements and forms. I glanced at the statements and noticed the Shimmerstone Investment Management logo on a large stack. The agent smiled at my paranoia.

"Sir, I haven't worked for Freedom for over two years," I said. The agent looked at Wyatt's face. His eyes were glued to the ground.

"It shows Fitzpatrick as the registered rep assigned to the account just two months ago." The agent pointed to his statement.

The judge beckoned the evidence to his stand.

"How can you account for this?"

I grabbed a statement with my cuffed hands. They were subaccounts at Shimmerstone I'd never heard of. I wanted to kill Wyatt.

"But you admit this was your account."

"It *was* my account, but I told you—I don't work there anymore."

"Your honor, we've subpoenaed Mr. Fitzpatrick's recent bank statements. There's a large wire for $450,000 to a bank in Spokane."

The half swinging door whacked open. It was Alice in her trademark tight-fitting sweater, ready to kick some ass. The judge pulled down his bifocals to get a better look at her.

"Your honor, that man is full of shit." Alice pointed at Wyatt.

"Young lady, you will address the court in a respectful manner."

"Sorry, your highness, but this man has caused me and my friends more trouble than you can imagine. I had to quit my job to keep from going to jail."

"You're saying that you committed a crime, too?"

Alice straightened her skirt. "Your honor, Jack did nothing except good clean business, except for that Lake Tahoe stuff."

"So you're willing to testify, and pay the consequences if you incriminate yourself?"

"You can bet the bare bottom under your robe, sir." Alice winked at him.

I reached my handcuffed hands around Alice and hugged her. If I broke *her* ribs, she'd just laugh about it. She put her freedom on the line for me. That was the ultimate friendship. I could never repay her.

"I'm naming my firstborn after you, Alice."

"Mr. Fitzpatrick, you are free to go, but you are not to leave the county for thirty days pending this investigation."

I hugged Alice again while the bailiff unlocked me, and closed my eyes, rocking her back and forth.

"Leave now, Mr. Fitzpatrick, before I change my mind. We have a busy docket."

I opened my eyes. She was here! Laila rose from her folding wooden auditorium seat, grinning from ear to ear.

"Who is that hot tamale?" Alice boomed.

"Hopefully my wife."

Laila batted her eyes at me, giving me hope. She extended her hand to Alice. I moved behind Laila to make her the meat in our hugging sandwich.

"Fitzpatrick. Now!"

# Chapter 49

# Freedom Fight

The state's investigation uncovered all of Wyatt's misdeeds, which started way before I moved to San Fran; that's when Wyatt contacted my client at Shimmerstone. He knew how much money I was making, and how I was doing it. But my guy wouldn't take Wyatt's phone call.

Emily, the sexy assistant, was long gone. She'd decided to go to veterinary school. But Wyatt kept calling until one day he was transferred to a new, less important portfolio manager. Wyatt explained to him how things might work if he didn't want to work up the ladder in the slow traditional way.

They started trading. After Freedom took its half, Wyatt would send a check with no printed address to the portfolio manager's house for his cut. Easy money—until the two dirtbags got in a fight. Wyatt was marking up the trades more than they agreed and got cut off. Then the portfolio manager found a new broker who agreed to give him more of a cut. Wyatt didn't care too much. By then he'd saved up enough to start trading his own account, betting on the market using imaginary accounts that had no assets. No need for splitting that way.

So he contacted me, and a few other Wall Street trading contacts, and started doing his deal: buying from one and selling to the other, until last week, Black Eye Friday. The day I hit Ling, and the day the economics number went the other way. Wyatt lost everything, and his brokerage accounts were seized to pay back the losses, at ten different firms, including the one we safekept for him.

In the end, it was the brokerage firm's fault for not knowing their customer, not Wyatt's for being a sleazebag. The courts used the same defense against the brokerage firms: "Buyer beware."

So what buttface did to me wasn't enough to put him in jail, but his splitting part *was*, because he didn't pay taxes.

Wyatt would have gotten away with it, if the sleazy portfolio manager's nosy receptionist wasn't eavesdropping. She turned him in after he snapped at her one day.

Wyatt agreed to squeal if he could get off with a lighter sentence— except he and the portfolio manager were the only ones who did anything wrong.

They were just two guys who got caught. I'm sure there were plenty more like them, defrauding investors of their rightful gains. Front row tickets to Madonna weren't enough for them.

Alice was banned from the security industry for a year, just like me, but she wasn't doing that anymore anyway. Wyatt wasn't quite so lucky—five years in jail and a fine equivalent to every penny he had.

I would have fought my suspension. I mean, after all, no profits were split with South Lake Tahoe. I just made more money than the account did. But the energy, plus lawyer fees to get me reinstated, weren't worth it. I was fried.

"Jack, do you ever think about moving to a quieter place? Having kids?" Laila asked, a week after it all went down.

"Maybe in ten years or so."

Laila looked out my apartment window and lowered her head.

I hugged her from behind.

"And you'd be more than my first choice when that time comes."

"What about six months from now?" she asked, patting her belly.

I spun her around.

"You're not fucking with me, are you?"

"That's how all this happened." Laila pointed to her belly and smiled. I loved her sense of humor.

I opened the patio door and hollered! "Ya-hoo!"

Then I panicked.

"I need a job." I called Dexter.

"Mate, you and I should become a team. We'd sell more copiers than anyone in town," he said.

But his job sounded awful to me. Not that there is anything wrong with hucking Xeroxes, but it just wasn't very glamorous.

"And your baby could go to that twenty-grand-a-year preschool down the street," he said.

"Which one?"

"That place in Pac Heights, where all the parents line up in their Range Rovers." I could just imagine.

To make ends meet to send my kid to grade school, Dexter and I would probably end up purposely offending anybody who didn't do or buy exactly what we wanted. We were getting too old. That wasn't funny anymore; it would just be scary, and now that I was going to be a dad, that kind of stuff would be extra creepy. I took a deep breath and called Mom.

"Mom?"

"Hi, honey!"

"I lost my job."

"That's okay dear, you'll get another one." This was a good part about Mom—never asking too many questions.

"What would you think if we came and lived with you for a while?"

"Who's *we*?"

"I'm getting married, Mom!"

"When?" she squealed.

"No date yet." I shrugged at Laila.

"Oh."

"And she's pregnant." A black hole sucked away the remaining zeal in her voice along with my breath.

"Honey, how did this happen?"

"A spaceship and some probing." More silence. "My snake, her grass."

"You know I haven't raised kids in quite a few years."

"You don't have to worry about that."

"How do you figure?" she asked, knowing very well I was full of shit. Couldn't she just suspend belief once in a while?

"Is it because you'll miss out on your beauty sleep?" San Francisco had taught me a politically correct way to win her over.

"We could get an apartment if you wanted, and let you live in the house alone." I made a face at Laila and covered the phone.

"Absolutely not," she said.

I put my finger over Laila's lips and nodded at her.

"When's the baby due?" Mom asked.

"About five months."

And so it was settled. Dexter had to find a new roommate.

I went to Green Valley to say good-bye, but it was empty, papers strewn everywhere. It wasn't like they boarded it up or anything, just nobody worked there anymore. All New York had to do was cut off the phones and hope someone would sublet the empty office from them.

I made a call to Darlene and found out Johnny moved to So. Cal. to surf; Deepak quit to import rugs with his brother; Noah was the lead volunteer team member at his kids' day care; Virginia was working in a Christian bookstore; and Darlene got hired by a megabroker back at Merrill and was making bucks. There was nothing holding me back from heading home.

## Chapter 50

# Tail between My Legs

It was late May when we left San Francisco, the same month I moved to LA. four years ago. We were headed home on the same I-5 that brought me so close to success.

Mrs. Pohkliss had won. How I dreaded seeing her face. My heart would stop if she told me that she "knew I'd be back."

I glanced in my side mirror at my U-Haul trailer. Anybody with just a little bit of money would use a moving company or even a drop-and-ship place. I deserved this punishment, this humiliation.

"It's so beautiful here," Laila commented as we passed through the Dalles, the armpit of the Columbia Gorge.

She'd slept through most of the good stuff. We passed Mount Shasta, through Bend and the red lava fields where the world gets its patio rocks, and past the snow-capped volcanoes, each staking out its ground a hundred miles from the other.

The Dalles might be a lot of things, but beautiful wasn't the right word for a dry, treeless wasteland. Beautiful compared to Kansas or something. I patted Laila's knee and kept trying to feed her positive attitude as we passed by a red-faced bearded guy fighting with his girlfriend on the highway shoulder in front of his white pick-up.

"You sure you don't want me to drive?" she asked.

"The roads are tricky up here," I said.

"Yeah. Just follow the signs on the four-lane highway to Spokane," she said as I rubbed our baby's head through her belly and smiled for a few more hours until finally we descended Sunset Hill into Spokane's unchanged skyline.

It made me sad—a different kind of sad than when I left. I felt sad that this was the best I could do. If I was single, I wouldn't even be getting laid with my sad story.

I put the Jeep in neutral and got it rolling about 70 mph past the faded blue and white "Spokane, a Great Place" billboard I'd seen a thousand times.

"Nice trailer! I knew you'd be back," the O in the billboard sneered at me.

"Fuck you, billboard. You're facing Airway Heights. You can't see the house I bought."

"Jack, who are you talking to?"

"That billboard?" I pointed to the sign.

"I knew you should have let me drive." Laila tried to look interested, observing her new city as we exited the freeway.

"It's so cute here. It's like time stopped," she said, glancing at a diner in the shape of a milk bottle. Lauren's face appeared, making me wince.

I took a deep breath and ignored her comment, turning the Jeep up Bernard Street to the South Hill. I turned right on Cliff Drive toward our new mansion and parked under a giant mature ash tree, excited to show her our new home in the Beverly Hills section of Spokangeles.

Mom wasn't home. She was at her annual outing with her friends at Hauser Lake. I was glad to have some time to get settled. I found her hide-a-key just where she told me it was.

"Check it out." I opened the front door, which was so heavy it could kill us both if it fell off its hinges.

"And the glass." I fondled the door until she nodded. "It's beveled. That costs extra."

The front room felt a lot like Mom's house up in Hillyard. Her modern taupe '60s couch (with matching ottoman) was centered as the focus of the room.

"Your father said this will be worth a lot of money some day," she'd always say before she knocked my tennis-shoed feet to the floor. The grand rooms made her furniture look child-sized.

"Why don't you take a nap," Laila encouraged.

No way. I was too amped. I drove Laila to Gonzaga the long way. We went along the river to avoid Division Street and the endless array of fast-food restaurants that made me feel ashamed.

"Ain't we living now. We've got fifteen McDonald's." I remembered Gramps shaking his head, driving past where his favorite diner was being ripped down to make way for a new Golden Arches.

"These big franchises think they're putting one over on us small-town folks," he added.

At first I didn't really understand what he meant, but I did now. The big guys were selling something, and we were buying it without really thinking about it, one unneeded franchise after the other, losing our homespun culture for the chance to make someone else a buck. That made us hicks.

I felt embarrassed Spokane wasn't secure enough in itself; people here thought they were missing out on what folks had, or thought they had, in the big city instead of just creating cool stuff on their own. But I loved Spokane! I loved Spokane!

A hundred years ago, they didn't worry about that. Spokane was the shit, the biggest city between Minneapolis and Seattle. People came from everywhere. The capital of the Inland Empire, where everyone saw the future and the beauty of what this place had to offer. They went ahead and built those big mansions on the hill. San Francisco had never lost its attraction. I was mad Spokane had. Mad this town wasn't enough for me. Mad it made me feel like if I didn't leave I was missing out on just about everything. That if I stayed I'd have to work in the basement at Nordstrom's because my dad didn't own a business. Mad I didn't have a dad to show me how to make money. I was going to teach my new baby everything I knew. I would play catch whenever the kid felt like it, until it was pitch black outside, and he'd get bonked between the eyes and go in crying to Laila.

"Jack, why don't I drop you off at home? You could go for a run. That'll make you feel better," Laila said at my sad face.

"I'll snap out of it; don't worry."

I ran through the lilacs in Manito Park, past the duck pond, toward Grand, where the awful crash happened on prom night. The city had since installed a 20 mph sign with a flashing yellow light in the exact location it happened. I guess that was something. I ran up to the sign and touched it and thought of my three friends who died that night. It was cold. I was still alive. Life *was* short. I was lucky that night. In the limo, Henry had pulled me inside and insisted it was his turn to stand up out of the sunroof, probably so he could be next to Lindsey. I looked up at the flashing yellow light. It was time for me to slow down. I was going to be a father soon. But slowing down had nothing to do with failure.

Back at the mansion, I was renewed to see my one treasure, Laila, the light of my life, the best thing I had to show from my travels. On the way to the kitchen, I floated past the mahogany wainscoted entry, running my finger along the top board to check how Mom was keeping up with the dust in this huge house. Not bad. I looked down. The gleaming wood floor should have been covered with expensive antique rugs.

Just then, a strange but familiar smell alarmed me. Like from the prison cafeteria, but not. Two pink Samsonites sat by the back door, sporting big yellow tags that read CLOSEOUT. I broke into a sweat, perspiring like a glass of iced tea in summer.

"Jack, ifs that ooo."

I ran to the sound in the dining room. There was Laila, holding a Whammy burger from Dick's in one hand, and stuffing her mouth with a glob of fries covered in tartar sauce with the other. How she was already hip enough to the local fast-food scene to pay the extra nickel for tartar sauce was a detail I found especially unnerving. I had to act fast. I slapped the burger from her hand. It bounced once on the floor.

"Omigod," she gasped, swallowing hard on her mouthful. "What are you doing? I got you one; relax," she said, pushing in another round of fries instead of taking a breath, forcing me to snatch the remaining grease sticks from the table and throw them in the trash.

"What is wrong with you!" she garbled.

"What is wrong with *you*? This stuff will kill you! Do you want cankles?" I would have been happier if I walked in on her banging the gardener. "You can't do this," I said to her, looking down at the oil-spotted bag.

"You, my friend are freaking out," she said. "I'm the pregnant one. I get the built-in wig-out credits, remember?"

She reached for the trash, but I blocked her way. Wrestling a hungry pregnant woman was a no-no, so I calmed her fire by resting her face on the outside of my shoulder and rocked her gently.

"Do you know what a Number Five is?" she mumbled with her mouth still full.

I held her sadly in front of me, watching her mouth chew before she forced the hamburger down. It was as if our future child just asked me, "Daddy, what's a bastard?"

"Well, do you?" she asked.

"Yes."

"Then what is it?"

"Who taught you this?"

"You don't know what it is, do you?"

"It's a cheeseburger with no onions, and it's not on the menu." Some ancient local customs, like the native Hawaiians throwing their retarded babies from cliffs, should probably always be kept a secret.

"I thought you'd be proud of me."

"No more Greasy Dick's for you!" I pushed her away and jumped up and down, stamping my feet in a tantrum.

"What did you say to me?!" She was pissed for real now.

That's what all the locals called Dick's burgers. People would still crack a smile when an old lady would comment in earnest, "Nothing like good ol' Greasy Dicks," before sitting down to chow a burger at one of the outside picnic tables.

Laila really didn't get it. This would be the end of her. The end of *us* if she continued! She was not going to be that kind of Spokanite!

"And the suitcases!" I kicked the pink rectangle clear down the hall.

"Aren't they hilarious? Value Village." She ran to hug the remaining one, petting it like a cute dog.

"Who told you about that place?" I ran over and checked inside it for bloodstains, just in case they were from that crazy vet.

"There is a reason no one will buy a pink suitcase in Spokane."

Laila sat down on the suitcase.

"We've got to talk," I said.

"You're scaring me."

"You can't just go around town and do this stuff."

"What? Eat a burger? Save you money on luggage?"

"Exactly."

The doorbell rang. It took twenty seconds to complete its melodic bongs.

"Don't go anywhere."

Laila crossed her arms, rolled her eyes and shook her head.

I opened the small-latched peep door. It was *her*. Not now. Not now.

"Good, you're home." Her needle nose and left eye took up the framed wrought iron square.

I closed the tiny door and quietly banged my forehead against the wood.

"Please go away; please go away," I whispered while she continued to knock.

"Jack, let me in. Why are you acting so strange?"

I heard her leather shoes finally shuffle down the brick walkway. Thank God. I could fix this later by feeding Mrs. P's ego, telling her I was so excited to see her I needed to take a shit right then. But I couldn't deal with this right now, not after the burger and the suitcases.

I took a deep breath and walked back to the kitchen, rubbing my eyes.

"Well, hello," Mrs. Pohlkiss said, letting herself in through my glass storm door. Her eyes fixed on Laila's baby-filled stomach.

"Jack didn't say he got married." She extended her hand to Laila without actually looking at her. How quickly she could invade my cells, cut me down, and make me feel like shit in seconds.

"We're not married yet." I put my arm around Laila.

"Does your mother know?"

"She was the first one we told."

"You know you can always get the birth certificate changed afterward to say you're married. So the child won't be a ..."

Mrs. Pohlkiss looked at the Dick's burger bag in the trash and then smiled pertly.

"If you decide to do that."

Laila wiped her greasy fingers on her smock. She was feeling the first pangs of Mrs. P's scorn.

"You two must come over. You can meet David, Charles's friend from Harvard. You've heard of Harvard, haven't you, dear?" Laila nodded like a half-wit.

"I didn't know Charles was back."

"It was only when your mother told me you were here that he even agreed to visit."

"How about tomorrow?" I asked.

"No, now. Charles loves surprises. He thinks I'm gone all day."

"Actually, Laila was just going to take a nap. Weren't you?" I cocked my head to the side and pleaded.

"Actually, I'm fine now," she said, moving closer to me. She whispered under her breath, "You shouldn't have thrown away my Number Five."

Mrs. P grabbed Laila's hand and headed for the door.

"Well, aren't you going to join us Jack?"

I should have just let Laila go alone, but it wasn't just her anymore. She was pregnant with my baby. Laila had no idea whose cloven hoof she was holding. Officially, everything had gone wrong today.

We walked down the path next to my row of hedges, toward Mrs. P's row of hedges. Mine looked better—healthier, more mature. Surely she must have noticed this. I ran my fingers through the robust leaves until Mrs. Pohlkiss looked back to take note.

"David has written a play that is being produced on Broadway." *Take that*, she said.

"That's terrific." Laila being an ass-kisser was not very becoming.

"What do you do, Laila?"

"Right now, not much." Laila patted her stomach.

"She's a lawyer. Graduated top of her class at Boalt." I blurted.

"Really? Maybe you can defend unwed mothers."

Laila looked at me to make sure she'd heard her right.

"What is going on with you two?" Laila whispered to me.

Around the front, near the mailbox, I noticed my brown "M" was gone. Mrs. P noticed my stare.

"The radon gas seems to be gone," I said.

"That's because I buy top of the line," she affirmed.

We continued on to the blue-gray flagstones of her back patio. She stopped at her kitchen door and put her finger to her lips before motioning us to walk behind her to the library.

"Where are they?" she whispered. We were surrounded by shelves of leather-bound hardbacks. "They were sitting here reading Shakespeare when I left. I just love Shakespeare, don't you?"

In unison, we all looked at the ceiling and listened like hunters to faint classical music coming through the furnace ducts.

"They must be downstairs."

We padded down to the basement, where Charles and I used to play pool for hours. We were constantly reminded that our dads loved to shoot pool together.

"Charles?" A sound of a wounded animal was muffled under cranked classical music that had lots of cymbals and drums. Laila looked concerned while Mrs. P felt the dark wall for the light switch.

There they were, lying face-down on the pool table. Charles had his hands tied to opposite corner pockets. David had his eyes closed and was riding on top of him, oblivious that the spotlights had been turned on to their stage.

Charles spun his head around, his eyes huge, grunting in absolute panic through his blue bandana gag.

"That's right, baby. And you said five inches was nothing." David slapped Charles's ass and banged even harder while Charles wriggled to free his bound hands in vain from the leather lattice pockets.

"No, you don't. Daddy's not done with you yet." David leaned down and breathed in his ear, which made Charles buck like he was being electrocuted.

David slapped his ass again.

Mrs. Pohlkiss jumped over and spanked David as hard as she could.

"Get off him!" Mrs. P screamed.

David shrieked and spun around, rolling off the table, grabbing a pillow off the couch to cover himself.

"Give me that." Mrs. P wrested her pillow from David, leaving only his hands for cover.

"These are dry clean only! Very expensive!" She shoved the pillow in front of Charles' face, pointing to the new body fluid stain, "You weren't raised like this."

"What's up, Charles?" I asked.

Charles shrugged. *Not much.* I reached down to shake two of his fingers through the webbing of the corner pocket.

"This is Laila."

"Don't you think you should untie him?" Laila said.

"Your body oils are ruining the felt!" Mrs. P. screamed.

"How's Boston?" I asked, trying my best to pretend this wasn't really happening.

Charles shrugged.

"It's great to see you, man."

"Me moo," Charles said through the gag while I fiddled to free him.

"Do you have a knife?" I looked over at David.

Mrs. P went over to the minibar and returned with a pristine cheap wood-handled steak knife. The kind you get for free when you open up a charge account at the Crescent. It had never been used before to cut limes for margaritas like it was supposed to be. With that thought, all of a sudden, I felt very sad for her. How had she wielded so much power over me?

"And what is this goop you've left on the felt!" she screamed.

Mrs. P picked up a penis-shaped bottle of Erota-Lube and pitched it at Charles's back in anger. Charles grunted and glared at her before turning back to me.

"Fagg-fagg," Charles grunted through the bandana.

"Dude. It's cool. I don't care. I kind of had a clue."

Charles shook his head and then banged his forehead on the felt. I moved the bandana off his lips.

"Jack. Thank God. Get the *gag* off me."

"Looks like you've been working out," I said, concentrating on cutting the ropes.

"Yeah, a little bit."

"David, these are some amazing knots you made," I said.

"Boy Scouts," David said.

Laila caught herself laughing and turned her face to the wall. I motioned her with my head to console Mrs. P.

"Everything is going to be okay," Laila said, putting her arm around Mrs. P.

"Why couldn't Charles be more like Jack?"

I couldn't believe what I was hearing. I had to stop cutting to absorb this.

"You know none of this matters," Laila said, splaying her hand at the naked spread-eagled Charles.

"Do you think that I didn't know? My Playgirls weren't just vanishing into thin air."

Mrs. Pohlkiss folded her arms in her familiar way and gazed at Charles. He looked around at her, his face finally relaxed. They loved each other, even now.

"Jack never needed anything. He worked for everything. No matter how tough it was. He never complained. He never cried. Not even about Montana."

I couldn't believe what I was hearing. Did she kill Montana to make me cry?

And then there was a bark, a tiny little bark, coming from over in the corner where a large blue kennel rested.

Mrs. P's shoulders rose to her ears, and her face bunched up. She started to cry. Laila rubbed her back. Mrs. P had one of those faces that was very unattractive when she cried. It just made me more uncomfortable. I had to go see where that little bark was coming from.

I pinched together the bar latch of the kennel and pulled out a helpless, adorable little chocolate-brown Labrador.

"Welcome home, Jack," Mrs. P said.

The puppy licked my nose like he'd been waiting for me all his life. He barked. I cried.

"Can someone please untie me?"

"Sorry, Charles." I put the dog on the pool table next to his face and let it lick him while I finished with the ropes.

All the hours I spent trying to prove something to Mrs. P—it was all for bullshit. I should really thank her. I never would have gone to seek my fortune if it wasn't for Mrs. P. Maybe that's what drives anyone to be successful. Trying to prove to a parent, or to a Mrs. Pohlkiss, or to that bully from fifth grade, or to that chick who didn't like you, or to a fat zit-headed trader that you are worth your weight in gold. But if it wasn't Mrs. P, it would have been someone else, or worse, nobody at all, when it should have been just me. And how do you get jealous and angry at yourself? I was growing up.

Laila grabbed a blanket off the couch and draped it over Charles. "Thanks."

"You sure pulled these knots tight, Charles," I said.

"Sorry."

"This doesn't have anything to do with me farting in your face?" I asked. Charles and I laughed.

Little Montana peed on the felt. Mrs. P just smiled.

"This calls for a celebration!" I walked with the knife toward Mrs. Pohlkiss. "Where are your limes?"

I made margaritas for everyone, and a virgin one for Laila. I cut the limes with her steak knife—like it was supposed to be used—and we laughed about my last few years. There was nothing to hide, even the part about Alain.

Those rich guys were right. Money can't buy happiness, because happiness is everywhere. It's free, like air. You can't bottle it like tequila, or take it in a pill. And no one can take it from you, either. It's inside of you, locked up by a key that only you hold. If you lose the key, you just have to find it again, because it's in there somewhere.

Everyone has a bag of shit to get over. I had no one else to blame for the things I did. All those freaks I met didn't bug the shit out of me: I *let* them bug the shit out of me because I was just like them.

I guess I really could be happy in a small town or even in no town at all. It all came down to whether I was comfortable in my own skin, and believed in the important things, such as love and friendship.

And so to you graduates of whatever school of hard knocks you're from, may you go out and prosper. Don't let the freaks you meet get you down. If you think you're going to fail, you'll never get out of bed. Which is what I have to do right now. I have an interview this morning at Nordstrom's—for a job on the main floor.